# GOURMET
# CORNWALL

# GOURMET CORNWALL

Carol Trewin

photography **Adam Woolfitt**

foreword Philippa Davenport

Alison Hodge

# contents

# foreword

I have had a soft spot for Cornwall since childhood. The first holiday I remember was spent there, a pebble's throw from a cove that might have inspired Daphne du Maurier's *Rebecca*. I remember the glorious light (the light that makes Cornwall a Mecca for artists). I remember mushrooming in cow pastures and potato fields, and gathering blackberries from hedgerows. And I remember feasting almost daily on fried mushrooms, and blackberry and apple pie with clotted cream.

Carol Trewin's heart-warming and eye-opening book feeds these memories, sets them in context and rounds them out with graphic detail. Supported by Adam Woolfitt's excellent photography, she explores the landscape, the history and the culture that has helped to shape the Cornish people, their lives and diet down the centuries. She traces the recent quiet evolution from modest backwater cooking to an honest modern cuisine that is rooted proudly in local produce. And she introduces key producers, movers and shakers of Cornish foods today.

Historically, Cornwall was England's poor relation county. The hard-won livelihoods of her fishing, farming and mining communities were further disadvantaged by Cornwall's distance from the rest of England, out on a western limb, until the advent of the railways and refrigeration opened up communications and fresh food export potential. Yet, even in the sixteenth century, enterprising Cornishmen sent tons of smoked and salted pilchards annually to France, Italy and Spain. So prized were these little fish in Spain, Carol informs us, that the Spanish name for them – *fumados* – was adopted by the Cornish, and became charmingly corrupted to 'fair maids'.

*Right:* Hell Bay Hotel, Bryher, Isles of Scilly.

Bringing food matters bang up to date, we are reminded that Cornwall is the home of England's only real food fast food – Cornish pasties. The PGI (Protected

Geographical Indication) status now being sought for them surely deserves to be granted. For the best Cornish Pasties are every bit as good as the best Neapolitan Pizza. And when this status is granted, Cornwall's place will be irrevocably secured on culinary world maps. Meanwhile, as the first in-depth study of contemporary food in Cornwall, this book should be treasured by visitors and locals alike.

Philippa Davenport

# introduction

Cornwall and the Isles of Scilly are many things to many people. The first daffodils in the dying months of winter; modern and vibrant as epitomized by the Eden Project and the surf culture of the North Cornwall coast; an extinct tin mining industry, represented by lonely chimney stacks and derelict engine houses; a soft-focus image of picturesque coves and harbours, which enchanted generations of artists – from Stanhope Forbes and Walter Langley, Barbara Hepworth and Ben Nicholson to Kurt Jackson – each still with its complement of bobbing fishing boats; the Royal Cornwall Agricultural Show at the height of summer.

Given the county's strong emphasis on tin mining and fishing, for hundreds of years farming, for the most part, was relegated to producing sufficient food to meet local needs. In the 1760s the historian and cleric Dr William Borlase wrote of Cornish mining that:

> If it exceeds much its present limits agriculture must decay; it is best therefore, to encourage both so that the former may promote plenty of money and the latter food and raiment, and both the happiness of that spot where they meet.

It is not surprising that until recently, with the exception of a few dishes and food stuffs, Cornwall has had a relatively simple food culture, focusing on dishes such as fish, bread, the Cornish pasty – which evolved as a miner's portable lunch, and used whatever ingredients were to hand in a poorly furnished kitchen – and occasional festive dishes, such as Stargazy Pie, which were served only for specific fairs, feast days or holidays.

*Right:* Early daffodils near Penzance.

Much has changed since Dr Borlase wrote almost 250 years ago, and despite the decline in British agriculture since the early 1990s, farming is more important in Cornwall than in many other counties. Fishing, although now only a tiny part of the county's economy, is still a vital element in its social structure and, like farming, is also under political and financial pressure.

Despite all this, a food renaissance has been quietly developing in the county, and while it would be unrealistic to imagine that this applies to everything grown, sold, processed, cooked and eaten in Cornwall, visitors are surprised by the quality and range of new Cornish food and drink on offer.

This book sets out to explore the links between contemporary Cornish food, the landscape, history and culture. It weaves its way around these four elements. It does not set out to be a definitive guide, but gives a personal snapshot of some of the best food businesses and producers in the county. Needless to say there will be ones that I have missed but should have included, others that have changed hands in the period between writing the book and publication, and those who, while brilliant, have sporadic bad patches which happen to be when the next keen foodie visits. So forgive me if I have overlooked your particular favourite.

Not long ago I suggested to a friend that we should have a 'Cornish' for supper. At first she did not quite understand what I was getting at. Well why not a Cornish? We often have an 'Indian' or a 'Chinese'. My theory was that we could eat an interesting and excellent supper featuring mainly Cornish produce – and we did, proving my point exactly. You could argue that it may have depended on non-Cornish recipes, but it was the quality of the Cornish ingredients – bread, cheese, the freshest of fish, wine and salad – that made it a truly memorable meal.

Until 140 years ago Cornwall was a poor county, with a working population of mainly miners, fishermen and farmers. There were, and still are, few large towns: there was a strong underlying chapel influence, and in the main it was a tough, rugged society that lived simply, on a poor diet. It was not a cuisine de luxe, but a diet that evolved out of availability and necessity. Undoubtedly, Isambard Kingdom Brunel's Royal Albert Bridge, built over the Tamar River to provide the final link in a joined-up railway system, changed that. But the underlying influences remain, which is why I have concentrated on the historical diet of the working families rather than the handful of wealthy landowners and aristocracy.

Perhaps the county's distance from London, and relative isolation, also meant that hints of feudalism stayed longer in Cornwall and the Isles of Scilly than in other rural counties. But at the same time it remains a deeply Celtic land – rugby, choral singing, the Gorsedd and brass bands epitomize its Celtic roots – linking it firmly to other Celtic nations such as Wales or Ireland rather than the rest of England. These pastimes also symbolize the hard life that many Cornish families once led – a far cry from the softer, contemporary occupations represented by computer screens, body boarding, arts and crafts, and tourism. Some of those arduous, tough industries survive – particularly sea fishing, the most hazardous occupation in the world.

In European monetary terms Cornwall remains a poor county, with less than 70 per cent of the average European GDP, which is why it has qualified for significant amounts of EU funding. But the county is rich in other ways and its heritage, culture and food are among those riches.

Things are far from perfect in Cornwall and the Isles of Scilly. Mining has been wiped out, farming and fishing are struggling, but there is much that is good and getting better. There is no doubt that not only does Cornwall

produce some of Britain's finest food, but there is more of it and it is improving all the time. Given the range of products available, and the high quality of the food cooked in pubs, restaurants and cafés, it is not surprising that the *Observer* recently voted Cornwall the best place for foodies in its series 'Ten Best Places to Be'.

While international chefs search for ever more obscure ingredients to put on our plates – think witchety bugs, bee larvae or sand crawlers – and others, such as Heston Blumenthal, push the boundaries of food combinations to the point where eating out is closer to an A-level chemistry exam than a food experience, chefs in Cornwall have rediscovered the freshness and quality of many simple but superb Cornish ingredients, which they are using as a platform to develop their own style of uncluttered, honest cuisine.

If the industrial revolution effectively dislocated most consumers from the land and from food production, this book is a modest attempt to restore that connection. It is also an attempt to draw the links between our modern preoccupations and their historical antecedents; to understand why Cornwall has such distinctive landscape features and social pursuits.

Take gigs, for instance. The gig once had a crucial function for pilots guiding ships into and out of difficult harbours. Shorter, narrower and faster than seine boats, at the height of the Cornish fishing industry and before the introduction of the combustion engine, they were well suited to hand-line fishing for mackerel, ling and hake, even seine netting for mullet. Now we think of them purely as racing and leisure boats.

So Cornwall has many elements: sea, coast, sun, golden sand, waves breaking on rocky shores, deep hidden river estuaries, rolling grassland, bleak granite moorland and prehistoric field

patterns. These are the things that determine Cornish food, and they in turn have been determined by thousands of years of growing, ploughing, grazing, fishing and smuggling.

Finally, a huge thank you to all the chefs, food producers and others in this book who so generously gave their time and expertise to help bring *Gourmet Cornwall* to life.

## a note on measurements

All recipe ingredients are given in metric quantities; otherwise I have used metric or imperial measurements, as seems appropriate in the context.

Carol Trewin
March 2005

*Top left:* The Cheesewring, near Liskeard.
*Bottom left:* Ancient field system, Zennor.
*Above:* Penzance women's gig team on their way to evening practice in *Senara*.

# 1 taste the sea

It is a wet bank holiday Monday in Looe. Not much doing, until suddenly a coach load of Japanese tourists takes over Pengelly's fish shop on the East Looe quayside. The Japanese pick over the fish – literally – sniffing, feeling and prodding. They then buy virtually the entire fresh-fish display – everything from scallops to mackerel, John Dory, monkfish and gurnard, so excited are they by the freshness and quality of what they see.

Angela and Jackie Pengelly are left almost speechless by the experience. It is a rare example that highlights different cultural approaches to fish. The Japanese are full on and know what they like and how to handle it. As the world's greatest sushi eaters they recognize that this fish meets their demanding standards for super-fresh, top quality fish. The British, mostly, are diffident and unsure, regarding fresh fish as something to be wary of.

We should not be surprised by the Japanese experience in Looe. Being tidal, the harbour is home to many small and medium-sized day boats that are usually away fishing for a maximum of 24 hours. The catch, when landed, is the freshest you can possibly get, in tip-top condition, and is highly sought after by the best chefs and restaurants, not just in Cornwall but across the country.

This latest generation running Pengelly's comes from a long line of boat-owning, fishing families that have been connected with Looe and the sea for hundreds of years. The two sisters stand out in a male-dominated industry as the only female buyers at Looe's fish auction, which is the second largest wholesale fish market in Cornwall and also handles the catches of boats from Mevagissey, Polperro and Torpoint. The majority of the fresh fish and shellfish that Angela and Jackie buy, process and sell is caught by the boats moored a few yards away. Pengelly's and the best Cornish fishmongers are the only way to buy fresh fish

*Right:* Japanese tourists at Pengelly's fish shop, East Looe.

*Above:* Angela Pengelly.

– landed that day, still bright, still smelling of sea and salt, and having travelled only a few yards from ship to shop.

In Cornwall you are never more than 16 miles from the sea, so I make no excuses for starting with three chapters on fish. After tin and copper mining, fishing was the county's most important industry and, for centuries, most Cornish families ate more fish than meat. Although the fishing industry is struggling – against political pressures of quotas, restricted days at sea, levels of fish stocks and the Common Fisheries Policy – this is nothing new: a quick trawl through Cornish history reveals that this industry has frequently had its peaks and troughs.

In 1858, the *West Briton* reported that 'considerable distress prevails among the hardy fishermen of Newlyn and Mousehole, and their families. This distress is owing to the failure of the drift fishery during the past year.' But only three years later, in 1861, the newspaper reported the bustle of activity in Newlyn as seven new fishing boats were built: 'The boats generally are fitted out for the coming spring mackerel fishery, which it is hoped, will be as successful as the catches during the past year.'

## stargazy pie

Not surprisingly for a maritime county, Cornwall has hundreds of fish-based legends and stories. The story of Tom Bawcock and stargazy pie is one of the best known. Stargazy (or starrey gazey) pie is a far cry from the sophisticated fish dishes created by chefs such as Rick Stein, or those in the county's three Michelin-starred restaurants – The Abbey in Penzance, The Black Pig in Rock and Ripleys in St Merryn. Nor does it compare with the fish we expect to be served in Cornish pubs or beach cafés – often simply cooked, but fresh and still tasting of the sea. Stargazy pie is a reminder of the hardships suffered by many Cornish fishing communities when food was scarce and bad weather stopped boats from going to sea. The legend tells how one winter, after weeks of stormy weather, the people of Mousehole were close to starvation. Eventually one brave fisherman, Tom Bawcock, put to sea in terrible conditions and returned with a catch big enough to feed the village for Christmas. Seven different types of fish were baked in a celebratory pie, with the heads showing through the pastry to prove that there were indeed fish inside. Versions of the legend, and recipe, vary: some say the fish were pilchards, others herring or mackerel, still others that the fish heads and tails should show through the pastry crust. The legend lives on when the pie is recreated each year at the Ship Inn, Mousehole on Tom Bawcock's Eve, 23 December.

With 326 miles of coastline and hundreds of tiny harbours and inlets, it is hardly surprising that Cornish fishing villages have appealed to artists, visitors and residents for hundreds of years.

Prehistoric fishing would have used spears, hooks and rudimentary traps, and lines cast from the shore. Later, as boats became bigger and more robust, the Cornish were among the first to sail long distances in pursuit of their quarry.

By the 1570s, Cornwall had a thriving export trade of pilchards (see Chapter 3) and other fish, particularly hake, to continental markets. In 1582 there were 2,000 seafaring men in Cornwall,

compared with 930 active fishermen in 2001. During Elizabeth I's reign, Cornish fishing was nationally important. Cornish boats were sailing to Newfoundland for cod, fishing for herring and pilchard in the home waters, and following the herring shoals as they moved up the British coast. Pilchard, mackerel and herring were the primary catches, supplemented by many other species and shellfish (see Chapter 2). During the next hundred years or so the Scillonians were also exporting large quantities of fish, including cod, ling, pollock, mackerel, sole, turbot and plaice, to France, Italy and Spain.

The coming of the railway and the availability of ice (see Chapter 7) were responsible for the start of a boom time for Cornish fishing. Once Brunel's bridge over the Tamar was completed in 1859, Cornwall had fast links to London and access to large urban markets for the first time, and within two years more than 1,000 tons of fresh fish were leaving the county each year, particularly herring, conger, hake, cod and mackerel. The mackerel fishery was transformed by this new market, and the fish no longer needed to be salted or cured to preserve it. Penzance, Newlyn and Looe prospered, but smaller fishing villages, without easy access to the railway, became isolated by the cost of transport, and most fish landed there was sold locally.

*Above:* A wet day in Looe.
*Below:* Spotted near the harbour in Looe.

The other factor that contributed both to the development and later the decline of the Cornish fishing industry was motive power. Steam-engined boats started to displace the drifter fleet, although it took the Cornish until the early 1900s – some 30 years after their east-coast competitors – to switch from sail to steam. The combustion engine swiftly followed, making it easier to catch larger fish such as cod, ling and hake. Not only could Cornish boats travel much further, but boats from other British and foreign ports moved into the warm, species-rich waters off Cornwall and the Isles of Scilly. With ice on board, trawlers could stay at sea for longer, but on their return they would bring huge gluts of fish to the market, forcing down prices.

Two world wars also left their mark on Cornish fishing. Boats were burnt or left to rot, and two generations of young fishermen were wiped out by the conflicts. In the last 50 years, advanced engineering and increasingly sophisticated gear and technology have played a significant part in rapid and universal changes in the industry. Enormous, foreign-registered, factory-style fishing vessels were built that could stay at sea for weeks on end, with giant nets indiscriminately scooping up every shape and size of fish from the seabed.

The majority of the Cornish fishing fleet is made up of smaller boats, tradition-ally known as inshore boats. In 2001, 559 vessels were registered in Cornwall, 425 of them under ten metres long, the rest mostly larger beam trawlers based in Newlyn, Looe, Padstow and Newquay.

The smaller boats tend to work inside the six-mile limit that protects Cornish waters, setting pots for shellfish, netting and using techniques such as long-lining or hand-lining; many switch gear to vary the methods and fish caught, all according to the season.

The overall national and international picture is not good, with bigger, faster boats chasing fewer fish, made worse for the local fleet as foreign boats are drawn away from over-fished areas to well-stocked waters around the Cornish coasts.

Then there is the issue of discards and by-catch. Although fishing methods like hand-lining can target specific species such as mackerel and bass, modern trawl nets are indiscriminate, which inevitably means that with each trawl other species are caught that cannot be sold – either because the boat's owner has exceeded quota, or because there is no market for it. No-one in the industry is happy with a system that requires the discard, or by-catch, to be thrown back into the sea.

Fishermen are not impressed with the scientific analysis of some stock levels, which frequently does not reflect what they find each time they put to sea. Monkfish, for instance, are thriving. Monkfish stocks are allegedly over-exploited, yet many fishermen told me that tons are thrown overboard as by-catch each year. By-catch cannot be legally landed, and as 'few fish survive after being hauled around a deck for a few hours and then being thrown back,' it is wasted. The morality of this conundrum of throwing away good, marketable fish seems highly questionable when thousands of people around the world are starving.

What makes it worse for Cornish boats is the fact that the rich western waters can be fished by foreign vessels, while they have to remain tied up in harbour because of quota restrictions. It is hard for trawler-owners to look at their capital sitting idle for half of the month, and little wonder that British fishermen question the logic of receiving government handouts paying fishermen with years of experience and expertise to leave the industry, while the Spanish government invests heavily in its fishing fleet.

In one of West Cornwall's last remaining net lofts, Chris Care repairs old nets and makes new ones. The net loft is over 200 years old, but many fear it will not be in the same use in another 100 years. Chris, a mild-mannered and egalitarian man, is clearly not a complainer. But his analysis of the crisis facing the industry is accurate: 'It's quotas, rules and regulations that are killing things off,' he explained. 'I have to have four certificates to set to sea: health and safety, sea safety, fire fighting and first aid. Of course safety is paramount, and the training is good

*Left:* Billy Bunn making a net in St Ives.

## fish in cornish waters

Cornwall's clean seas are host to a rich variety of fish and shellfish. Some of the 50 different species landed in Cornwall include:

- Bream
- Brill
- Cod
- Coley
- Conger eel
- Dab
- Dover sole
- Grey mullet
- Gurnard
- Haddock
- Hake
- Herring
- John Dory
- Lemon sole
- Ling
- Mackerel
- Megrim sole
- Monkfish

- Pilchard
- Plaice
- Pollock
- Red mullet
- Sea bass
- Shark
- Skate
- Turbot
- Whiting

- Crab
- Crawfish
- Cuttlefish
- Lobster
- Scallop
- Spider crab
- Squid

because it makes you more aware of potential dangers. But some of this just goes too far and makes it too difficult.' He returned to fishing after a career in the Royal Navy and mining at South Crofty, Cornwall's last tin mine, and works a day boat out of Hayle, catching mostly flat fish such as ray, lemon and megrim soles, and plaice.

He believes that fishing will survive, but shares the widespread concern that few of the next generation are keen to join an industry that is apparently in terminal decline, and which is the most hazardous and physically demanding profession. Long days and nights, much time away from home, and working against the two most unpredictable elements – the sea and the weather – fishing requires a hardiness and toughness of character that are becoming rare commodities.

Yet despite this gloomy prognosis, others in the industry are equally positive. Visit any of the dozens of tiny ports and inlets on the Cornish coast, and at the right time of year there is plenty of fishing activity. While Newlyn is the county's largest fishing port, boats of all shapes and sizes still put to sea from the smaller harbours – from Polperro down the coast to Cadgwith, Porthleven, Sennen, and further north to St Agnes and Boscastle.

Where the Cornish fishing industry scores over its rivals is its proximity to key fishing grounds, rich with more than 50 different species, which means the fish can be landed faster, fresher and in better condition than in other parts of the country. Newlyn, the premier English fishing port, is at the heart of Cornwall's fishing industry. It has a rightly deserved reputation for high-quality fish and shellfish, although up to 70 per cent of the catch is exported, mostly to Europe.

From a foodie's point of view, this is fish heaven: visit Newlyn and it is almost impossible not to buy fresh fish. A number of fish merchants have shops, and others are geared up for consumers to walk in off the street. Walk up the Coombe and you can buy freshly cooked crab from W. Harvey & Sons, or pop in to Robin Turner's unit for some scallops. Landed that morning, they could not be fresher, and the cleaning time allows you to hear the fishermen's latest preoccupations at first hand. Visit the town at the end of August when the Newlyn Fish Festival brings out the entire community in celebration of the many facets of Cornish fish and fishing. The sun shines, male-voice choirs sing as only Cornish male-voice choirs can; craftsmen weave willow lobster pots; Michelin-starred chefs cook squid and fish soup, and trawler skippers barbecue fresh Cornish sardines for thousands of hungry, greedy and eager visitors. Here we see the real fabric of this tightly knit Cornish fishing community – the gig crews and the naked fishermen who enthusiastically pose each year for the Duchy Quota company's calendar to raise funds to help the next generation of young fishermen – and get a sense of how it is bound together by the sea, and the inexorably increasing political pressures, to keep the industry and these communities alive.

In a town where almost the entire community goes to sea or works in one of the downstream and upstream fishing-industry support or processing businesses, it is no wonder Newlyn is so focused on fish, with landings auctioned through the market valued at £20 million a year. Without Newlyn, its boats, market, fish merchants and wholesalers, the Cornish fishing industry would not be as vibrant as it manages to be.

*Left:* Display at Newlyn Fish Festival.
*Above:* Fresh pilchards.
*Below:* Newlyn Male Choir.
*Bottom:* Cooked squid.
*Pages 22–3:* A fishing boat leaves Newlyn harbour at dawn.

Since the mid-1990s, Cornish fishermen have responded to the crisis facing some fish stocks and are promoting fish caught by smaller boats using more sustainable fishing methods – for instance, line-caught mackerel and sea bass. Chefs and restaurateurs are doing their bit too: the fish varieties served have changed considerably. Not so long ago, red and grey mullet would have been thought to be inedible, but now they feature on menus in the smartest restaurants, along with John Dory and gurnard. Increasingly, Cornish fish is taking pride of place on menus, and is being promoted for what it is: fresh, high-quality, and tasting fantastic – and all these things because it is Cornish.

Men like Gareth Eddy – who was born and brought up in a Cornish fishing village and cares passionately about the industry, having worked in it himself before becoming a chef – deliberately select fish that are from sustainable stocks or do not have quota restrictions. Fish and chip shops are responding to the challenge too, offering other fish in addition to cod and haddock – one Newlyn fryer offers a three-fish special, based on the day's landings.

Rick Stein has done more than almost any other television chef to promote fish as a wonderful, fresh ingredient that is simple to cook and, above all, tastes superb when in prime condition. Customers at his fish and chip shop in Padstow (eat in or take away) can select from a wide range of fresh, mostly Cornish fish, which is either cooked in batter or griddled, served with sublime homemade accompaniments such as aioli or curry sauce. Designed as an affordable, fishy alternative to Stein's Seafood Restaurant, it is interesting that more than half the sales are still of traditionally popular fish such as cod and haddock.

There's no doubt that without Rick Stein, the renaissance of interest in fish, not just Cornish fish, would have been far slower. He is the food hero of the moment to whom the entire Cornish fishing industry owes a huge thank you.

One man who is convinced there is a good future for Cornish fishing, and is extremely buoyant about it, is Matthew Stevens, whose father held the last fish auction in St Ives, later settting up M. Stevens & Son to sell fish landed by the St Ives fishermen. Matthew Stevens still buys direct from a handful of St Ives skippers, and also from Looe and Newlyn. Mindful of the problems facing the industry, he has strict ethical and environmental policies about the fish he sells, and was one of the first fish merchants to sell only local, line-caught mackerel and sea bass.

The business has grown considerably from its original shop, which has one of the best wet-fish displays in the county – adding a purpose-built factory on the edge of St Ives in the late 1990s. Here fish and shellfish are processed and prepared for sale to top hotels, shops, restaurants and mail-order customers across the country, with further expansion underway. Staff numbers have grown from five to 35, evidence enough, said Matthew Stevens, that Cornish fish stocks are healthy.

'I could not be doing this without the product,' he said. 'We would not be investing in the future if we thought it was unsustainable.'

The recognition of the importance of eating fish from sustainable sources, as part of a healthy diet has undoubtedly boosted domestic sales. Fish is no longer restricted to being one of the key ingredients in fish and chips. Nor is it just a fashionable food served in

*Top left:* Unloading the catch, Newlyn.
*Bottom left:* Fish market, Newlyn.
*Below:* Rick Stein's fish and chip shop, Padstow.
*Bottom:* Seen at Newlyn Fish Festival.

THE HERRING EXPERIENCE
PASSION CREATES POSSIBILITY

NO GUTTING IN HARBOUR BY ORDER Harbourmaster

restaurants. Fishmongers and processors are taking the pain out of the preparation, making it easier for us to cook and eat fish at home.

Personally, I can think of little better than buying just-landed fish or shellfish direct from fishermen in small coves and harbours like Cadgwith and Port Isaac, but if scaling, filleting and gutting is not your thing, Cornwall's excellent fishmongers – although they are declining nationally, the county has more than its rightful share of excellent fish shops, run by men and women with long links to the sea – will take the scariness out of preparing fresh fish.

Trelawney Fish, on the Strand in Newlyn, stands out with its fishy mural, and in addition to its own just-landed fish sells a comprehensive range of almost every ingredient you need for a fish dish, and has the recipe books to inspire you. Next door is Stevensons' wet-fish shop, run by the owners of Newlyn's biggest fishing fleet. In Porthleven, John Strike's Quayside Fish is well worth a visit, and there are similar specialist wet-fish shops up the coast from St Agnes to Port Isaac and Bude, all of which make the quality of fish on supermarket fish counters look like a third-rate product.

The start of the twenty-first century is a critical time for the Cornish fishing industry. Although boats continue to be decommissioned, and the debate about the level of fish stocks continues, there is a sense of optimism in Cornish fishing villages and harbours, and an underlying belief that Cornish fish has a sustainable and profitable future. Cornish fish are the stars in Cornwall's new-found role as a Mecca for foodies, and have become an essential part of the tourist experience.

Fishing may now make only a tiny financial contribution to the Cornish economy, but psychologically and emotionally the Cornish are drawn to the sea in an extraordinary way. The tightly knit fishing communities, where bad weather means no sailing, which in turn means no income, have an unspoken sense of unity. Tied together

by the sea, wind and weather they help to make Cornwall the
special place that it is. Sea fishing is the last element of our
hunter-gatherer culture that has evolved through thousands of
years of history and is a crucial part of Cornwall and Cornish
culture. There are none braver, or more generous in spirit, than
the county's fishing people. Lose fishing and you take the spirit
out of Cornwall.

*Top left:* Mural at Trelawney
Fish, Newlyn.
*Bottom left:* Filleting fish at
M. Stevens & Sons, St Ives.
*Top:* M. Stevens & Sons
fishmonger's shop.
*Above:* Matthew Stevens.

Most of the recipes in *Gourmet Cornwall* have been generously supplied by some of the county's finest chefs, all of whom, without exception, follow the same principles, using the best local ingredients where possible.

Sea bass has become a popular fish, but brings controversy in its wake because of some of the more industrial, pair-trawling methods used to catch it – mostly by French and Scottish fishing boats – which trap and kill dolphins. The alternative is to buy only wild, line-caught bass (farmed sea bass is also available). Many fish processors and retailers, as well as chefs, have started to clearly label the origins of sea bass and how it is caught.

# line-caught wild sea bass with orange, dill and green peppercorn sauce

'We are proud to say that all the ingredients needed to prepare this menu come from our local purveyors, fishermen and farmers, right here in glorious Cornwall,' is how Nick Barclay of Barclay House in Looe sets out his food philosophy. Like many other leading contemporary chefs in Cornwall, he is passionate about using and promoting good Cornish food. Working in Looe means that he can take advantage of the fresh fish landed by the harbour's fleet of day boats.

*Above:* Nick Barclay.
*Below:* Barclay House, Looe.

## ingredients

*Serves 4*

For the sauce
- 300 ml fresh orange juice
- 75 ml dry Cornish white wine
- 1 level tspn green peppercorns (in brine, not dried)
- 200 ml double cream
- 85 g butter

For the fish
- 4 fillets of wild line-caught sea bass – 200–225 g fillets
- 16 orange segments and confit zest
- 1 small bunch of dill, chopped
- 4 sprigs fresh dill
- olive oil for cooking
- salt, black pepper and plain flour for seasoning

## method

*Sauce:* Place orange juice and white wine in a saucepan and reduce by three-quarters to a syrup. Add cream, reduce by half, whisk in butter which has been roughly cut up into small cubes, add green peppercorns and season with salt and pepper. Set aside, keeping warm. If sauce is too thick, thin with a little water. If too thin, reduce a little.

*Fish:* Take the four bass fillets and remove any remaining bones. Season with salt and pepper and dust lightly with plain flour.

Sauté fillets in olive oil, skin side down first, to golden brown; turn over carefully and sauté until golden brown. A couple of minutes on each side should do it, depending on thickness. Keep warm.

Bring the reserved sauce almost back to a boil, and add the chopped dill just before serving.

Place a fillet on each plate, skin side up. Pour the sauce around the fish and garnish with orange segments, orange confit and a sprig of dill on top.

*Note:* Orange confit is orange rind that has been thinly cut into strips, blanched in boiling water, refreshed then simmered in sugared water to sweeten the rind and preserve it.

# 2 ropes and pots

On the corner where the sandy track turns 90 degrees and runs towards the bay, is a small blue and white painted sign on the wall outside a stone cottage:

**LOCAL SHELLFISH**
LOBSTER LIVE OR COOKED
CRAB WHOLE OR PICKED
PLEASE ENQUIRE AT TOP OF PATH

There are few places in the world where you can get fresher shellfish than on Bryher in the Isles of Scilly. Caught in the seas around the island, then cooked and processed before being delivered to the Hell Bay Hotel (see page 7) just 200 yards away, this is surely one of the best ways to eat fresh, local, seasonal produce. Perched on the far side of the island, this most westerly hotel in the British Isles has staggering views and fantastic food. What makes it special is not only the island location – which means a 48-hour delay between ordering anything from mainland Cornwall and its arrival – but that an increasing amount of the food is so local that it could practically have walked to the kitchens. Fresh Bryher crab is just one example, lobster another.

The Pender brothers, John and Mike, known locally as Pots Pender, have been catching, cooking and preparing crabs and lobsters for as long as anyone can remember. Local gossip suggests that, like many other Scillonians, the Pender family has been tangled up with fish and shellfish for centuries. Like so many islanders, they have easy access to plentiful crabs, lobsters and other shellfish in the clear blue waters only yards from their door, and the Hell Bay Hotel, passing tourists and other island hotels, cafés and restaurants are among their customers.

*Right:* Crabs at M & R Crabs, Newlyn.

Few people outside the islands are aware of the quality and abundance of Scillonian shellfish – it was a revelation to me on my last visit to discover one of the islands' best-kept secrets. There has been a considerable culture shift bringing fish back into prominence in the last few years, and local demand has boomed for fish or shellfish harvested from the healthy stocks around the Isles of Scilly. Although a lack of facilities to land and process fish prevents the islands from having a truly commercial fishing industry, an increasing number of independent fishermen, either line-fishing or setting pots for shellfish, have recognized the growing interest in eating the best quality fish, and have linked that to the islands' key industry – tourism. Of the 32 fishing boats working the clear, unpolluted and beautiful waters around the islands, 31 are inshore potters. More than half the crabs and lobsters landed go straight to mainland fish merchants in Newlyn; most of the rest are sold to local pubs and hotels – the perfect example of avoiding excessive food miles. This means that lucky tourists and islanders can experience this fantastic, local shellfish, often lifted from the sea just a few hours earlier.

*Above:* A sign on Bryher, Isles of Scilly.
*Below:* Buying crabs on the beach at Cadgwith.

Mark Pender, son of Mike Pender but living on nearby St Martin's, runs an on-line Internet shellfish business to take full advantage of the demand for fresh,

traceable shellfish. The Isles of Scilly Shellfish Company has an incredibly informative website, with all you need to know about cooking and dealing with lobsters, crawfish and crabs, which are shipped to customers (either live or cooked). Mark and his wife Suzanne are confident about prospects for this fledgling business, as more consumers seek out high quality seafood with history and pedigree, fished in a sustainable way.

'People in England don't eat enough shellfish, but we hope it's beginning to change,' Suzanne Pender said. 'People like Rick Stein with his food heroes, restaurants like FishWorks and Loch Fyne are all helping to promote the image of fish and shellfish.'

Most shellfish – crustaceans, single-shelled and bivalves – are regarded as gourmet foods, particularly lobsters, crabs, oysters and crawfish; others, such as mussels and prawns, perhaps less so. For hundreds of years shellfish were a luxury food, destined only for the most affluent dining tables. Here's how the Cornish social historian

A.K. Hamilton Jenkin records nineteenth-century fishing methods and the social differentials for shellfish:

> Crabs, lobsters, and crayfish were also dragged out of the rocks with crooks at low spring tides. These, however, were generally sold to the gentry, or more recently to the London markets, being considered 'too good' for people. The latter, however, made much use of the small shellfish, especially cockles and mussels, which were often preserved in vinegar.

And limpets too, when times were really hard. Not much change there then – except perhaps the limpets – even cockles and winkles have become something of a delicacy.

While overall fish landings in Cornwall have been declining, this is not true for shellfish, which make up almost one-third of the fish landed each year. In the breakdown of the catch into pelagic fish (fish found in relatively shallow water, such as mackerel and sardines), prime fish (sole, lemon sole, turbot, brill, bass) and medium-value fish (plaice, monkfish, megrim sole, cod, hake), shellfish take the biggest share at 33 per cent.

*Top:* Fish sale at Cadgwith.
*Above:* Fisherman at Cadgwith.

Non-quota shellfish – scallops, crabs, cuttlefish, squids, lobsters and crawfish – have become increasingly important to the Cornish fishing industry, a good earner for the small-boat, inshore fishing fleets. Since the mid-1980s, the number of crab and lobster pots has doubled if not trebled, and other boats fishing for different species, such as ray and turbot, often catch shellfish as a by-catch. As there is no quota for shellfish there are none of the associated by-catch problems either.

Cornwall and the Isles of Scilly produce some of the best shellfish in the world, but despite the large volumes landed in Cornish ports and fishing villages, only a small amount makes its way into local or national restaurants, often without anything to declare its Cornishness or its top-class provenance. Even less finds its way into the kitchens of knowing British consumers. Most of it – up to 80 per cent of species such as crab – is exported to France, Spain and Portugal, some of it live in special salt-water holding tanks, but increasingly as a processed product. Why is it that many of us enjoy crab or lobster on holiday abroad, but won't eat it at home? The irony is that these same shellfish, which seem so appealing when we are chilling out in warmer countries, have probably come from Britain.

*Above:* Lobsters at Looe.
*Top right:* Boiled crabs at M & R Crabs, Newlyn.
*Bottom right:* Hand-picking crabs at M & R Crabs.

If you can't manage the thought of buying your crab as soon as it is landed, direct from fishermen as they haul their boats on to the beach in coves like Cadgwith, then calling at one of the processors when the crabs have recently come out of the boiler is the next best thing. While crabs are almost invariably sold cooked, most lobsters used to be sold live, but a growing number of Cornish fish businesses are making them more accessible by selling both species cooked and dressed – in fishmongers, by mail order or over the Internet. Mark Pender on St Martins is one of the latest to start trading this way; others include Martin's Seafresh, Dennis Knight in Port Isaac and W. Harvey & Sons in Newlyn. Like most of the county's best shellfish processing companies, M & R Crabs pick theirs by hand, convinced that while intensely laborious, the quality of hand-picked crab is far superior to crab that has been industrially sucked and blown from its shell.

Jeff Martin, of Martin's Seafresh (a mail-order business in St Columb), a former fisherman turned online fish entrepreneur, makes it his mission to sell the freshest fish and shellfish to his customers, preferably within 24 hours of landing. He is convinced that Cornish shellfish is unbeatable in terms of quality and taste. Cornish lobsters, he says, benefit from the clean, rocky coastline where they thrive on the

North Cornwall coast, compared with the muddy waters in which Canadian lobsters grow. He points out that it is American and Canadian lobsters, often held in tanks or pounds for weeks prior to being flown live to the UK, which have flooded a limited market and created year-round availability.

Perhaps more than anything else it is the lobster that reminds us that most fish and shellfish are the last truly wild stocks that we hunt and consume. The lobsters' particular habits – solitary, slow-growing, aggressive and cannibalistic – and the non-intensive way that they are fished, are perhaps why they are so expensive compared with farmed salmon or mass-produced poultry. That is what makes lobsters a truly gourmet food, to be savoured and enjoyed for the superb taste and texture, in their limited season, when funds allow.

Other crustacea, such as oysters, share that exclusivity, strengthened by their seasonality and the difficulties of managing and harvesting wild stocks. In Cornwall the long history of oysters can be traced back thousands of years to the Phoenicians; oysters were enthusiastically consumed by the Romans, and have been fished in and around the county for over 2,000 years.

It is curious to think that native oysters, *Ostrea edulis*, which for many today are the ultimate gastronomic experience, were once the food of the poor. In the Middle Ages they were one of the cheapest foods available. In 1561 Tamar River oysters sold in Saltash for 2d (less than 1p) per 100. It was Dr Johnson who famously fed oysters to his sick cat in the eighteenth century, and less than a hundred years later, in *Great Expectations*, Charles Dickens described oysters as food for the poor. Within 20 years pollution and over-fishing had reversed this, and oysters achieved the luxury status they still have today.

Although they still grow freely in the upper reaches of the Fal, Helford, Percuil and Tamar rivers, the Fal and Helford fisheries are the last remaining areas in Cornwall where wild native oysters are harvested commercially. They may be one of the county's most prized gourmet foods, and perhaps one of their attractions, apart from the distinctive texture and flavour, is that the skills needed to manage the fisheries have

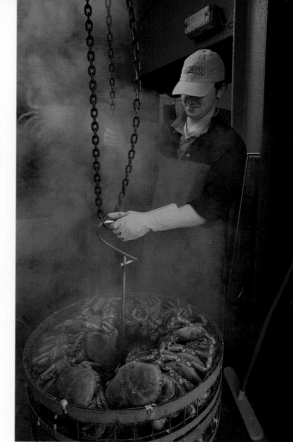

hardly changed for hundreds of years. Working the Fal and Helford oyster beds combines harvesting wild oysters with on-growing spats – young oysters which spawn naturally in the wild. Some are left to grow undisturbed, others are lifted and re-laid on the final fattening grounds.

Since at least the 1950s, these tiny fisheries have struggled to stay alive against significant odds including pollution, disease and other man-made environmental pressures, and while stocks look healthy, making a living this way is not easy. The fishery survives because it is carefully regulated. The season runs from 1 October to 31 March, and only licensed boats can fish, although the number of licences fluctuates each year. In the 2004–5 season the Truro Harbour Office issued 40 licences, but in 1914, just before the outbreak of the First World War, 229 boats, employing 487 men, fished for oysters on the Fal. Then as now, most were exported to continental Europe.

*Left:* Oysters at the Falmouth Oyster Festival. *Above:* Hugh Fearnley-Whittingstall at the Falmouth Oyster Fesatival.

The Fal is the last remaining oyster fishery in England where no motive power is used for fishing. The bivalves are dredged either by sail-powered boats up to 28 feet long, or by hand-winched punts, usually no more than 15 feet in length. Les Angell, a lifetime fisherman on the river described the technique:

> The dredge is like a metal knife with a mesh or net at the bottom and a top net, and we only work in certain areas of the Fal estuary. The act of dredging requires fishermen to go with the wind and tide, you do a dredge then you turn the boat round and start again, as the tide alters you go a different way.

It is a slow, painstaking process, as the dredge has to be lifted and emptied regularly. It may be hard work, but it conserves the fishery through its relative inefficiency. Any oyster that is undersized (two and five-eighths of an inch diameter) can be returned to the river bed to grow on.

Martin Laity is the latest generation of a handful of families left on the Fal fishery who have been part of this industry for almost 200 years. As well as fishing for

and cultivating oysters, he acts as a merchant for most of the other oyster fishermen, exporting the vast majority of their catch, though the tiny quantities he sells
to Cornish restaurants (less than 16 stone a year) are gradually increasing. Despite
occasional fluctuations in stocks, he is confident that there are healthy levels of
spats to provide a promising harvest in three or four years' time, when they reach
a marketable size, and that the oyster beds will survive.

Watching the fishermen working the beds on the River Fal has a sense of
timelessness that would be our loss if it declined irrevocably. But the older men
recall the days when oysters could be found all over the foreshore at low tide,
along with cockles, mussels, winkles and whelks. They acknowledge that even
this unique and tiny wild oyster fishery is not immune to the long-term effects of
marine pollution, global over-fishing and the impact that these have on the sea,
fish and shellfish stocks.

Native oysters, of course, can only be harvested and consumed between
September and April. But for all-year round supplies, Pacific oysters, *Ostrea
gigantea*, are farmed in Cornwall, although not yet on a significant scale. There
are farms at Rock on the River Camel and on the Fowey River.

The annual Falmouth Oyster Festival marks the start of the oyster season, and
continues to celebrate this rare Cornish delicacy and this unique part of Cornwall's
fishing heritage. It is the only time when the working boats are tested at their full
sailing capacity, pitted against each other and the elements, in the working-boat
races. Oysters are confined to a small, highly specialist market, so to consume
10,000 oysters during the four-day festival is some achievement. Love them or
hate them, they are a unique food experience. Oyster-lovers argue that nothing
else comes close to their delicate taste sensation: fresh from the shell, delicious,
a real taste of the sea.

Infinitely more popular and more widely consumed than oysters are mussels,
which have grown in the wild around Cornish coasts and in river estuaries for
centuries. Like cockles and winkles, they would have been a staple food for many
Cornish working families who could gather them at low tide. Farming Cornish
mussels is a recent innovation, where the bivalves are either grown on ropes or
dredged from river beds. Gary Rawle, of Fowey Sea Farms, uses ropes attached to
buoys on the Fal near the King Harry Ferry, later harvesting and moving the mussels to Fowey, where they are hardened off before purification and sale. At certain
times of the year he also dredges a limited quantity from the river bed.

Unlike farmed fish, these bivalves do not have to be fed in the conventional
way; they are filter feeders, consuming plankton and other nutrients from the water
as they breathe. This is a highly efficient, environmentally sustainable system when
compared with farming salmon, which need about three times their weight in

*Left: Rebecca*, skippered by
Phil Slater, takes part in the
annual working-boat races at
the Falmouth Oyster Festival.
*Pages 40–41:* Farming
mussels at Fowey Sea Farms
on the Fal.

fish feed to grow to maturity. Once in the Fowey River, the mussels are hardened off on oyster racks as they become accustomed to the greater tidal flow. The blue mussel, *Mytilus edulis*, according to Gary Rawle, has good, succulent meat and although rope cultivation has given it a reputation for having a delicate shell, it thrives in the Cornish river estuaries.

Traditionally most UK mussel farming took place in Scotland and Ireland. But Cornwall is catching up fast, and others are setting up in competition against Gary Rawle and his partner Dave Hancock, who also grows oysters, both native and Pacific, on the Fowey River. After ten years this relatively young business is producing about 100 tonnes of mussels a year and has no problem selling them, mostly to local merchants, with some going to national wholesalers and the rest to local restaurants.

Cornish shellfish takes some beating, but is largely unappreciated by most of us. What could be better, at the right time of year, than a plate of freshly cooked shellfish of your choice – crab, lobster or mussels – served with a glass of crisp, chilled, white Cornish wine?

# bryher crab with yoghurt and lime and crisp cured salmon

This recipe comes from Graham Shone at the Hell Bay Hotel on Bryher, in the Isles of Scilly. He is part of the team that has adopted the philosophy of using local produce to enhance the dining excellence that is becoming a key part of any stay on the Isles of Scilly.

## ingredients

*Serves 4 as a starter*

- 500 g fresh Bryher crab (roughly 80% white meat, 20% brown)
- 50 g chopped coriander
- 3 tbsps plain yoghurt
- 2 limes
- 12 fresh baby spinach leaves
- 100 ml virgin olive oil
- 50 g Cornish smoked salmon
- handful of fresh basil

Roasted tomato dressing
- 8 cherry tomatoes
- 1 clove garlic, chopped
- tsp chopped fresh thyme
- salt and freshly ground black pepper

Yogurt and lime dressing
- 2 tbsps lime juice
- 4 tbsps plain yoghurt

*Above:* Graham Shone.
*Below:* On the terrace at the Hell Bay Hotel, Bryher.

## method

Dry the cherry tomatoes with chopped garlic, thyme and seasoning in a cool oven (100°C, gas 1 or lower) for about an hour. Blend with a little olive oil if necessary to make a dressing.

Mix the crab meat with the yoghurt, adding lime juice to taste. Add the chopped coriander to the crab mixture.

Wash the spinach, dry and dress it.

Cut smoked salmon into strips and deep-fry in oil until crispy.

Lay three pieces of spinach on each plate then, using a 5 cm ring or a small pastry cutter, press the crab mixture in firmly until full, and press down gently to firm the mould filling.

Blend basil with olive oil to make dressing.

Mix together yogurt and lime juice. Place a small dollop of this dressing on top of the crab, and garnish with deep-fried salmon strips.

Drizzle the basil oil gently around on the plate, followed by the roasted tomato dressing.

# 3 salt, smoke and sardines

Fish have been cured since man started catching them. For thousands of years the only ways of preserving them were by drying – either wind-drying, or hanging them near a fire, which perhaps inadvertently became the first experimental smoked fish – or salting. The Celts were salting fish in 600 BC, and as salt became more widely available this became the main form of preservation in Cornwall and the Isles of Scilly. Salting took two forms: dry salting or curing in brine.

The Romans used smoking as a way of preserving goods – cheeses and wines were smoked to make sure they survived the long journeys to the furthest corners of the Roman Empire. Later, the techniques became more widely used for meat, bacon and some fish which, in medieval times, would be hung in fireplaces and left to smoke gently, preserving it for the long, dark winter months.

In 1602, Richard Carew, in his *Survey of Cornwall*, described Cornish fishermen using various methods of drying, salting, brining or pickling hake, ray, whiting, conger, mackerel, mullet, bass, salmon, trout, eel and turbot. For hundreds of years the Cornish cured pilchard, herring, mackerel, ling, whiting and dogfish, and dried and smoked bream, hake, cod, skate and ray. Smoked, salted and dried fish were easier to pack and transport around the country, particularly to areas away from the coast.

From a twenty-first century perspective, it is hard to believe that pilchard seining and curing dominated Cornish fishing for more than 400 years, and while these small, silvery fish were often the main source of protein for many Cornish

*Right:* Pilchards, salted and packed in a barrel, at The Pilchard Works, Newlyn.

families, the bulk of each catch was exported, as recorded by the great historian William Camden in *Britannia*, in 1586:

> They make likewise a gainful trade in those little fishes they call *Pylchards* which are seen upon the sea coasts, as it were in great swarms, from July to November. These they catch, garbage, salt, smoak, barrel, press, and so send them in great numbers to France Spain and Italy where they are a welcome commodity and named *Fumados*.

The first recorded exports were in 1555, and during the next 300 years, when not disrupted by war, this trade generated huge amounts of income for Cornish ports and fishing villages. Driven by religious diktats to eat fish on Fridays, and only fish during Lent, these Catholic countries consumed thousands of tonnes of salted pilchards a year, particularly in rural areas and during the winter. Some of the pilchards were also smoked after being salted; the Spanish were avid customers of these *fumados* – which, in Cornwall, became corrupted to 'fair maids'.

At the fishery's height, pilchards were caught along almost the entire length of the Cornish coast, from Cawsand in the South East, through Mevagissey and Polkerris, around Lizard Point, past Land's End and up the north coast to Boscastle.

The season lasted from June or July to December as the shoals migrated south and west. Almost every cove and harbour had its own pilchard cellars (or pilchard palaces) where the fish were cleaned, stacked, salted, and later packed into barrels, pressed and exported. The scale of the industry was such that not only fishermen and their families but almost the entire community was linked to this thriving trade, including merchants, rope makers, sail makers, boat builders and coopers. The pilchard provided food, money and light, for the oil obtained from pressing the fish was burnt in lamps.

Pilchards were mostly caught in shallow, inland waters by seining – a method that could hold great shoals of fish in the water for several days if necessary, until the catch could be landed – or by drift netters further out to sea.

Cyril Noall described the 'shooting' of a pilchard seine as a 'beautiful thing to watch, involving the exercise of great skill, judgement and team work by the fishermen, and carried out with the strategy and precision of a military operation'. It was also an event of frenetic activity involving every man, woman and child in the neighbourhood.

During the seining season, most of the seine boats would be on permanent standby, moored just off the coast, waiting for the pilchard shoals to arrive. They generally relied on the 'huer', on dry land, to spot the shoals and direct them to where to cast the seine nets. The cry 'Hevva, hevva' was the signal that a shoal had arrived, for the crews to start fishing and the rest of the community to prepare for the work ahead once the catch had been landed. Directed by the huer, the boats would row frantically to the correct spot, cast their nets and slowly draw in the shoal, either drawing the seine nets into the shore or holding the fish in the nets further off the beach. Tuck nets were then used to draw the fish to the surface, and baskets to scoop them into boats called dippers that landed them, whence they would be rushed to the pilchard cellars and 'bulked up'. This was the job of the women, helped by children, who cleaned and then layered the fish with salt, where they would stay for three or four weeks before being packed into barrels and pressed to extract more oil.

*Above:* Traditional salted pilchards ready for export to Italy at The Pilchard Works, Newlyn.

The romance of pilchard seining caught the attention of travellers, writers and commentators from Daniel Defoe to Wilkie Collins, who visited St Ives in 1851 and noted that the women were paid 3d. (just over 1p) per hour, and every six hours were given a tot of brandy and some bread and cheese. But a traveller to Mevagissey in 1793 probably had a more realistic view of what was, after all, an industry that relied on brief periods of very intense work in unpleasant conditions, that were usually wet, smelly and often cold. He described the village as the most wretched and disagreeable place he had ever visited:

The streets were all nauseous and offensive to a great degree.
For this was the season of the year for catching pilchards, and during
the operation of curing the fish, a very fetid oil arises from them.

Pilchard seining, like the rest of the fishing industry and Cornish mining, suffered years of boom and bust, feast and famine. In 1847, 40,883 hogsheads of pilchards were exported – estimated to be 122 million fish. In 1871, what started as a promising season, with some of the best catches ever recorded, turned into a dismal year for the seiners as the glut of fish flooded the market, prices collapsed, hundreds of barrels were returned from Italy, and many of the fish ended up being used as fertilizer.

A perennial problem for the curers was the punitive salt tax, and although fishermen officially received a duty-free salt allowance, it is not surprising that large quantities of salt were regularly smuggled into Cornwall. Court records show hundreds of prosecutions against shipping companies who 'lost' large portions of their salt cargoes 'due to bad weather', when much of the cargo was probably unofficially diverted elsewhere.

Many Cornish families relied on salting thousands of pilchards each year, which they stored in bussas – large earthenware jars – to feed themselves during the winter. But even in years when fish were cheap, the price of salt often prevented the poorest people from laying down sufficient stocks of fish. This problem was particularly acute during the Napoleonic Wars, when supplies of French salt – thought to be the best for the process – were cut off. In 1809, salt rose from 1d. per lb (about 1/2p per 454 g) to 4d. per lb (almost 2p per 454 g), making the cost of salting and storing a thousand fish £1. 3s. 4d. (£1.17), which was out of the question for a labourer earning only 6s. (30p) a week. The salt duty was not removed until 1825.

Why did the pilchard industry decline? There are many theories, but the most likely explanation is the combination of the railway, ice and refrigeration techniques, and bigger, more powerful boats that could sail further and made a wider range of fish species available all year round. The railways could deliver fresh fish, packed in ice, to London markets and other inland towns and cities within 24 hours of its being landed. Curing and preserving were no longer needed for pilchards, mackerels, herrings or other fish, even though in 1873 the Home Office set up a pilchard canning factory in Mevagissey.

The combination of declining markets, and the effects of two world wars on an industry that was rapidly shrinking, ended what had once been the mainstay of Cornish fishing. By the 1950s, the pilchard had become an outmoded, unpopular, old-fashioned food, mostly available canned in tomato sauce.

*Left:* Terry Tonkin at The Pilchard Works, Newlyn.

When Nick Howell took over the Pilchard Works in Newlyn in 1980, it was the last traditional pilchard curing business in Britain, selling into a declining market. Without his vision and enthusiasm, pilchards would probably have disappeared from British kitchens altogether. *Sardina pilchardus* is, in fact, a mature sardine and Nick Howell, spotting that the sardine had considerably more allure and cachet than its adult form, rescued it from obscurity and revived the humble pilchard's fortunes by reinventing the 'Cornish sardine'. Cornish sardines have become a star attraction in fish restaurants; fresh sardines can be found in most Cornish wet fish shops, and in many supermarkets.

*Below:* The Pilchard Works, Newlyn.
*Bottom:* Atlantis Smoked Fish, Grampound.

The Pilchard Works – open to the public as a working museum – still produces traditionally salted pilchards and a range of pilchard/sardine-based products fitting contemporary cooking needs and styles, in many cases making an excellent substitute for anchovies, and with not a tomato in sight.

Further up the county it is hard to miss the roadside signs outside Atlantis Smoked Fish in Grampound. The bright, fluorescent yellow signs beckon you in for fresh local crabmeat and oak-smoked fish, and once inside the tiny, higgledy piggledy shop you quickly recognize that this is a shrine to all things smokey, particularly fish. An impressive range of more than 20 smoked products includes smoked mussels, prawns, mackerel, hot-smoked salmon tails, smoked cod roe, smoked eel, kippers, smoked haddock, cod, and hot-smoked salmon.

Atlantis Smoked Fish is one of a handful of dedicated fish-smoking businesses that appeared in Cornwall in the 1970s. It was the abundant shoals of mackerel

in the 1970s that kick-started Cornwall's stand-alone, artisan smoked fish industry, when some savvy entrepreneurs recognized that this was an opportunity to add value to this under-rated fish that would otherwise have ended up exported to Eastern Europe, or as fertilizer and livestock feed. Although this was good for smoked fish businesses, it was bad news for the mackerel. This was the time of the Klondikers – large Russian factory ships that moored just outside the six-mile fishing limit and swallowed up millions of tonnes of the fish, putting huge pressures on mackerel stocks, which have never fully recovered.

Although fish processors and merchants had continued smoking cod, haddock, herring and other fish, it was mostly to preserve gluts when particular species were abundant, and became less important when the railway arrived. Many fishermen had small wooden or brick-built smokehouses of their own. At the end of the nineteenth century, fishing ports like St Ives had a number of smokehouses, almost entirely dedicated to smoking herring for kippers, which would be run by Scottish or Irish women, who moved down the country following the shoals of fish. But until the 1970s, speciality smoked fish had been the preserve of the London smokehouses, for salmon, and Scotland and the North of England – home of kippers, Arbroath smokies, and buckling – where legend claims that John Woodger developed the modern herring curing and smoking process in Seahouses, Northumberland in 1843.

Martin Pumphrey, at the Cornish Smoked Fish Company (now part of Westcountry Smokehouses), was one of the first in Cornwall to set up a dedicated craft business smoking mackerel, starting initially with whole smoked fish, using a Dutch method. Filleting followed later, as the fashion grew for smoked mackerel as a 'modern' delicacy served in hotels and restaurants. Things have moved on since then, and smoked fish (and other products including meat and cheese) appear in many guises, although it is oily fish, such as mackerel, herring and salmon, that really lend themselves to the process that turns them into a speciality product. Personally, I see little value in smoking foods that don't need dressing up – for instance, scallops. Exciting though a smoked scallop sounds, why bother to muck about with something that depends on its simple, delicate freshness to make it a wonderful eating experience?

The growing vogue for smoked fish also inevitably led to an industrialization of the techniques, where artificial dyes and added smoke flavours are used as short cuts to speed up the smoking process, and to improve profits but not necessarily the product. This, and the development of large-scale fish farming, particularly salmon, have made smoked salmon widely available and affordable in supermarkets, and in doing so have moved us away from appreciating the real delicacy and taste of properly smoked, properly produced (i.e. wild) fish. Salmon has suffered a reverse process of the oyster story, changing from being an exclusive, seasonal dish to being widely available in supermarkets all year round.

*Top:* Smoking herring for kippers.
*Above:* The Kipper House. Both seen at Newlyn Fish Festival.

Fortunately, no salmon is farmed in Cornwall and the county's dedicated artisan fish smokers still use traditional methods. Their kilns may now be stainless steel rather than brick, but they are built on the same principle that allows a draft of air to gently surround the products.

If you want some good, traditionally cured and smoked fish, Cornish producers are among the best – as the numerous awards won by businesses like Cornish Cuisine and the Tregida Smokehouse testify. Tregida, a relatively young business which started selling its first products in 2000, is stocked by prestigious London shops such as the Bluebird store in Chelsea and Villandry in Great Portland Street, and in Waitrose. Based in North Cornwall, the three partners have combined traditional smoking techniques with the latest technology, using stainless steel kilns that can be managed to provide consistency of product regardless of external influences such as the weather. The range of products includes smoked mackerel, smoked salmon and smoked trout, kippers and smoked haddock.

Further south, on a small creek on the side of the River Fal, you can find Cornish Cuisine, one of the smallest commercial smokehouses in England, which has been smoking Cornish fish for more than 20 years. Father and son Nigel and Jude Ekins are great craftsmen, using traditional methods to create foods with flavour and a good appearance.

'Modern machines take the art out, and produce bland food that is a combination of dye and smoke flavour,' Nigel explained. Some woods, he continued, give a wonderful patina to the food but do nothing for the taste. Others – oak, for example – can overwhelm the taste of some foods. He prefers a variable blend of other woods that might include walnut, apple, chestnut and cherry to give a lighter and more subtle flavour.

The Ekins use the draft method of smoking, in which the smoke is carefully drawn across the food, so that it is not damaged by high temperatures. In many cases this also makes for a long, slow process lasting several hours, needing constant attention to maintain consistent levels of smoke and temperature, which

*Top left:* Smoked mackerel at Tregida Smokehouse. *Below left:* Anne-Marie Hambly packing smoked mackerel at Tregida Smokehouse.

## smoking

Smoking techniques have changed little over the last 1,000 or so years, except that, as in every other facet of modern food production, the old tried and tested systems such as open chimneys and brick kilns have been replaced or updated by modern, often stainless steel, smoking cupboards. Fortunately for good food lovers, the best artisan producers have found ways of adapting the new technology to the traditional methods, ending up with a product that maintains its flavour and quality while keeping the Environmental Health Officers happy too.

There are two types of smoking – hot smoking and cold smoking. But before smoking, the fish has to be cured, usually either by soaking in a brine solution, or dry cured by sprinkling with salt, and sometimes sugar. Curing draws out excess moisture making the flesh more able to absorb the smokiness, while the smoking adds flavour and colour and preserves the fish.

Cold smoking is a slow process, at temperatures between 20° and 30°C, and can take anything between 20 and 36 hours, depending on the ambient temperature and the product in question. As the drafts of air are drawn slowly across the foods, a subtle flavour is built up. There is a fine art to getting the temperature right – too high and it seals the surface before the smoke has penetrated the meat or fish.

Hot smoking, for foods such as hot-smoked mackerel and hot-roast salmon, also for poultry products, cooks the food at the same time as adding flavour and works at higher temperatures, ranging from 72° to 85°C and sometimes higher, taking anything between two and six hours, again depending on the product.

In the past, probably any type of wood was used, more often than not the off-cuts from boat-building and other timber trades. Now the emphasis is on selecting the precise wood for the purpose. Most smokers use hardwoods like oak or beech, others, such as Nigel Ekins, choose aromatic fruit woods that impart their own particular flavour. A question of horses for courses – or a tree for every occasion?

may mean that Jude or Nigel can be found carefully tending the kilns in the early hours of the morning.

The Ekins are keen to support local fishermen and fish wholesalers, so as much fish as possible is sourced locally and is determined by availability and seasonality. Nigel Ekins is adamant that mackerel can only be smoked during the winter and spring, since during the summer the fish have insufficient oil. If Cornish herrings are not available he will not produce kippers. Such is the enthusiasm and passion of this tiny team that you feel that anything edible might just end up being smoked in their kilns.

*Left:* Nigel Ekins with a tray of freshly smoked trout at Cornish Cuisine, Penryn.
*Above:* Jude Ekins prepares trout.
*Below:* Shavings of fruit woods are used for smoking at Cornish Cuisine.

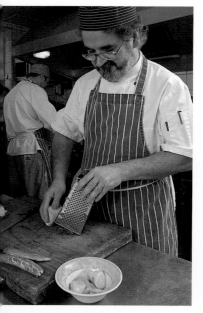

# seared scallops with smoked mackerel and horseradish cream

Smoked mackerel is probably one of the most widely available smoked fishes. This recipe from Mike Maguire at the award-winning Trengilly Wartha near Constantine, gives a new twist to a popular ingredient. Like all the other Cornish chefs featured in this book, Mike is an enthusiastic champion of local and seasonal produce, which is reflected in the changing menu at this popular gastropub.

## ingredients

*Serves 4 as main course*

- 24 scallops, cleaned and in half shells if possible
- 50 ml olive oil
- 1 heaped dessert spoon of freshly grated horseradish
- 200 g crème fraiche
- half a small Savoy cabbage
- 1 smoked mackerel fillet
- salt and black pepper for seasoning

## method

Discard the outer leaves of the cabbage; wash the rest in plenty of cold water, and drain. Shred the cabbage and then sweat it in a saucepan with half of the oil.

Add the horseradish to the crème fraiche.

Briefly sear the scallops in the remaining half of the olive oil.

Put the scallops in a warm oven along with the cleaned half shells.

Heat the crème fraiche and horseradish mixture, and fold in the cabbage.

Finely dice the smoked mackerel and add half to the crème fraiche mixture. Season to taste.

Divide and spoon the mixture

between the scallop shells, and place the scallops on the mixture. Sprinkle the rest of the smoked mackerel on to the scallops and serve. (Alternatively, serve on the cabbage mixture in large soup plates, without the scallop shells.)

*Top:* Mike Maguire.
*Above:* Trengilly Wartha.

# 4 black and gold

A splash of blue catches your eye as you drive through South East Cornwall in July and August, the flowers not of woad, that ancient source of blue dye, nor linseed, once grown extensively to collect European Union subsidies under the Common Agricultural Policy, but of lupin. 'Why lupins?' Ian Lobb's customers ask him. The answer is that growing lupins is the only way he and his brothers, Terry and Richard, can guarantee that their farm has a source of non-genetically modified protein to feed their beef cattle and sheep. As Ian put it: 'Customers make the connection and it gives them confidence in the product. Quality and confidence are very important.' The Lobb brothers, and a number of other top Cornish butchers, are continuing a tradition of farmer-butchers that has grown up over centuries of rearing and selling animals. These are men and women who understand that the best meat is achieved through knowing the animals, their producers, and the breeding and rearing methods, and following this through from farm gate to plate, using traditional, old-fashioned methods of maturing, hanging and butchery – skills that have been finely honed for generations. The difference between meat produced, finished and butchered in this way, and meat that has been mass-produced in semi-industrial conditions – quickly slaughtered and processed for a fast return – is almost indescribable: textures and flavours are simply incomparable.

On Kestle Farm, next to The Lost Gardens of Heligan, the Lobbs show how modern food production continues to shape the Cornish landscape. The 842-acre farm managed by the three brothers is an example of traditional Cornish mixed farming at its best. The countryside in midsummer is stunning – a patchwork of different greens, yellows, blues and ochres. The small fields, all with their ancient names – Higher and Lower Paradise, Almshouses or Lower Blow the Winds – are

surrounded by hedges full of flowers and wildlife, and there are numerous small copses of ancient deciduous trees. Beef cattle and sheep graze meadows humming with bees and butterflies. It is almost too perfect to be true. But the farm is a twenty-first-century business, not an exercise in nostalgia, and demonstrates how it is possible to continue the best traditional methods while responding to contemporary demands and concerns: hence the lupins, both blue and yellow, and a small crop of sunflowers. The South Devon or Limousin-cross suckler cattle are fed a mixture of grass, hay, silage, maize, barley and milled lupins. The result is tender, succulent beef raised in an extensive farming system run in total harmony with nature – a combination of wildlife conservation and commercial farming.

Five generations of Lobbs have farmed this land and, like many other British farmers, the current generation has found it hard to continue farming sustainably and profitably while remaining sensitive to the natural environment. The three brothers decided that the solution was to add more value to their own livestock, and to cut down food miles by using a local abattoir and selling beef and lamb from their new farm shop. All the other meat they sell is also sourced as locally as possible. This decision has not only guaranteed their survival but helps other local farmers to stay in business as well. Meat produced by the Lobbs is of superb quality and provenance – food that consumers can trust. In many ways the Lobbs' philosophy, as stated in their farm interpretation centre, is quintessentially

what this book is about: 'It is important to the future of the Cornish landscape that we encourage people to be aware of the connection between the countryside we cherish and the food we eat.'

Cornwall's tradition of producing top-quality livestock for the table and for local consumption is, in historic terms, relatively new, although the Cornish have been rearing livestock for thousands of years. In about 2400BC the early Bronze Age settlers built small enclosures for growing cereal crops and some winter fodder, while the uplands were heavily grazed during the summer. The tiny fields (similar to the field patterns still to be seen in Penwith) would have had granite or slate hedges, or earth banks and ditches, both the forerunners of what is known as the traditional Cornish hedge. The grazing animals would have included sheep, goats, pigs and cattle, used mostly for their milk, wool, and sturdiness as working animals. Rearing animals for meat was less important, the meat usually being produced when the animals

*Above:* A field of lupins at Kestle Farm.
*Below:* Sheep and small copses of ancient deciduous trees, in South East Cornwall.

were culled at the end of their working life, or in late autumn when there was insufficient fodder to feed them through the winter. Until well after the Middle Ages most Cornish peasants existed on a poor diet of bread, pottage (made from oats, barley or dried beans, flavoured with vegetables – leeks, onions, kale and herbs), fish (for those close to the coast), vegetables, and whatever wild food they could hunt, poach or scavenge. This would include seals, sea birds (puffins, shags, sanderlings and gulls) and rabbits, which had been introduced from France to the Isles of Scilly as a farmed species in the twelfth century, but subsequently escaped and naturalized in the wild. Dairy produce (see Chapters 5 and 6) did not play a major part in the diet either. Cattle were used mostly as work animals; sheep primarily for wool and then for their milk (which would have been made into cheese or butter); and goats for milk and a little meat, particularly in West Cornwall, where goat husbandry thrived until the end of the eighteenth century. Despite improvements in farming and livestock-rearing methods, meat barely figured in the average Cornishman's diet until Victorian times, and could only be afforded by wealthy landowners and the clergy.

By 1602, when Richard Carew published his *Survey of Cornwall*, cattle and sheep farming were becoming more widespread, and attempts were being made to improve the quality of the livestock. However, grasslands in the north of the county, noted as good areas for summer grazing, were hardly used by Cornish farmers: 'In times past the Cornish people gave themselves principally ... to the seeking of tin, and neglected husbandry, so as the neighbours of Devon and Somerset shires hired their pastures at a rent and stored them with their own cattle', Carew observed.

The 1789 bread riots in Truro, which coincided with the start of the French Revolution, epitomized the continuing

## feasting

Meat was not widely eaten by the majority of the Cornish population until the late nineteenth century, and many recipes have survived showing how adept the Cornish were at making do with a minimum of meat (see Chapter 9 for more on Cornish pasties). Muggety pie, using obscure offal cuts (pigs' intestines or sheep's pluck), or Taddago pie, using prematurely born piglets, featured predominantly in Cornish kitchens. Another popular dish was Cornish under roast, where the meat was cooked, either in strips or as a whole joint, under potatoes and vegetables. This was easy to cook in kitchens where the cooking arrangements were rudimentary – usually just a simple hot iron plate over an open fire, until the first Cornish range was introduced in the 1880s.

Although meat was not eaten frequently, it was always plentiful on Cornish feast days and at festivals. A.K. Hamilton Jenkin describes how a prosperous mining family in St Just feasted at the beginning of the nineteenth century: while cottagers were unable to celebrate on the scale of the farmers or yeomen, 'every household at that time kept up the feast to the utmost limit of its means.' On this occasion, when the stewing crock was finally lifted off the fire it contained: 'a rump of beef, a couple of fowls, and a nice piece of streaky pork to eat with them; as well as turnips, carrots, and other vegetables, all in kipps (net bags) to keep them separate and for convenience in taking up.' The feast also included a rabbit pie, a plum pudding and potatoes, and would have been followed by brandy and a hot toddy 'to settle the stomach'.

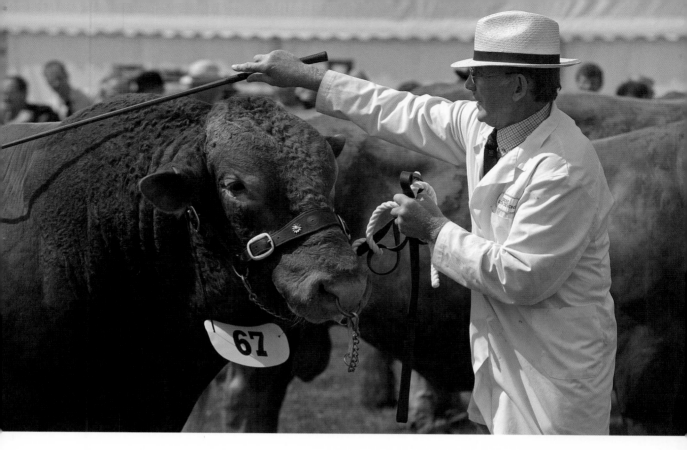

*Above:* Judging South Devon bulls at the Royal Cornwall Show, near Wadebridge.

food supply dilemma facing the majority of Cornish people. This and many of the food riots during the next 60 years were caused either by wars fought elsewhere – food produced in the county had to supply the army and navy as a priority – or by merchants and traders who recognized that they could sell for higher prices out of the county. By the early nineteenth century, the poorest Cornish families' diet had barely altered for 300 years. A.K. Hamilton Jenkin describes a scanty diet based mainly on potatoes and pilchards:

> Broth or soup, made from vegetables and a few meat bones, was looked upon as the best dinner of the week, and on that account was reserved for Sundays. On other days, the dinner of a working man generally consisted of nothing better than a slice or two of bread and treacle, or at best a barley pasty containing only potatoes and turnips.

The one source of meat widely available to most of the rural population was pork. For hundreds of years most cottagers or peasants had a pig, fed on waste and scraps. A fortunate few would also have had some hens and other poultry. This continued in rural Cornwall until after the Second World War, and many older people still recall the ritual and excitement of killing the pig. Neighbours and all the family would be involved, helping with the scrubbing, boiling, salting and

*Top:* Ian Lentern.
*Middle:* Philip Warren.
*Bottom:* Margaret Warren
keeps the books straight.

other work needed to ensure that not a single part of the animal was wasted. For many cottagers this was the only meat they ever tasted: half of the carcase would be eaten fresh, the other half preserved or cured – salted or smoked, made into sausages, brawn, souse (ears, cheeks, trotters and snout pickled in brine or ale) and white and black pudding. However, the high price of salt, until the salt tax was abolished in 1825, often meant that half the pig had to be sold to buy enough salt to cure the remaining half.

Meat production continued to grow, but little was destined for Cornish tables – a situation that hardly changed until the end of the nineteenth century. Although the quality and quantity of meat produced in Cornwall improved, most of it was sold out of the county – being sent either to the Navy's victualling yards in Falmouth or Plymouth, or, after the construction of Brunel's Royal Albert Bridge over the River Tamar, to the increasingly prosperous middle classes in the expanding English cities. (See also Chapter 11.) It seems ironic that, in the twenty-first century, pig production has almost disappeared in Cornwall, reduced to a handful of specialist producers, many with small breeding herds, whereas lamb and beef are two of Cornwall's biggest farming sectors. Although meat and poultry have replaced fish as the main source of protein in almost everyone's diet, a large percentage of meat produced in Cornwall is still 'exported' out of the county. In 2002 Cornwall produced 19,700 tonnes of beef but consumed only 8,200 tonnes, and 5,000 tonnes of lamb and mutton, only 3,100 tonnes of which was eaten in the county. The mild, damp climate and long summers create good conditions for growing grass which, until after the Second World War, when artificial fertilizers and manufactured animal feeds became widely available, gave Cornish farmers a competitive advantage.

As tin and copper mining declined, Cornish agriculture developed and became more efficient. For centuries, mining had been so dominant that great areas of land had been left undeveloped, as there was every likelihood that they would be seized for mining. Even if given up after the mines were exhausted, the land was left littered with detritus and scarred with abandoned shafts, and with the soil and watercourses poisoned by arsenic, sulphur and other mining by-products. With the exception of south-eastern Cornwall, where the china clay industry continues to have an impact on the landscape, in other parts of the county where tin and copper mining were less dominant, enclosure and cultivation of new land steadily increased during the late eighteenth and throughout the nineteenth centuries, creating what we take for granted today as the 'natural' landscape – a mixture of pasture and cereal-growing areas.

It cannot have been an easy period for Cornish farmers, though: just as the industry was evolving, miners and their families – the primary local market – were emigrating *en masse*, and those left behind were still too poor to be able to afford meat. Without improved transport links, the rising affluence of the urban bourgeoisie as industry grew and prospered elsewhere in England, and the new popularity of the county as a holiday resort, livestock production in Cornwall would have declined rapidly. It was at this point that some of the county's longest-standing butchers were established. These include Vivian Olds of St Just – more than 100 years old and currently run by the fourth and fifth generations, Christine Olds and her son Randall – and Philip Warren in Launceston. Both these follow the farmer-butcher tradition, as do Ian Lentern in Penzance and Ralph Michell at Higher Callenick near Truro, rearing much of their own stock or buying from local producers with whom they work closely on production systems and the breed of animals used. These master butchers have a huge advantage over other meat retailers: they understand the breeding and rearing as much as the butchery and retail process, a guarantee that anything you buy from these men and women will be of the finest quality and flavour, and of proper Cornish provenance.

'You are shopping at one of Britain's best butchers' reads the sign in the window of a Launceston butcher's shop. Philip Warren & Son (and wife and daughter)

*Above and below:* Philip Warren & Son, Launceston.

is probably the biggest single butchery establishment in the South West, certainly in Cornwall. Inside the shop it is easy to see why Philip Warren has achieved a reputation for being one of the country's best artisan butchers: everything is cut and prepared on the premises and all the products are fully traceable back to source. More than 3,000 customers travel to Launceston each week, so that even on a mid-week morning the shop is constantly busy and the 30 staff (including 24 fully trained butchers, almost all taught their trade by Philip) are buzzing around the chillers and cutting rooms behind the shop, keeping the meat counters replenished and preparing orders.

Philip Warren epitomizes the grazier-butcher: a farmer himself, he places great emphasis on sourcing the rest of his meat from farmers and producers in the locality with whom he has long-standing working relationships. Beef, particularly, comes from within a few miles of the shop, pigs and sheep from slightly further afield. He also specializes in selling rare-breed pigs, lambs and cattle, wild venison and excellent poultry and game.

Seasonality is very important, so some products vary throughout the year. 'We can't be all things to all people, but it's hard work getting some chefs to understand seasonality,' he said, voicing an as yet unresolved frustration that I heard frequently from chefs and producers alike. 'This part of North Cornwall is a tremendous fattening ground for cattle,' he explained. He concentrates on selling traditional breeds that are grass-fed and naturally reared. Devon, South Devon, Hereford and Aberdeen Angus cattle provide the beef, although he admitted to a personal partiality for Dexter beef, raised and fed in the traditional way. The carcases are hung for a minimum of three weeks, before being butchered into a range of traditional beef cuts. Philip believes that it is a combination of breed, rearing, slaughtering and hanging that creates the best eating sensation. 'No one used to talk about the eating quality, but that is something we have followed for the last 25 years. Now it's coming back into fashion again,' he said. The business also cures its own bacon and has a range of award-winning sausages, 1.5 tonnes of which are sold each week. High quality is essential, so occasionally some items are not local – gammons from Denmark are an example, simply because they are, in his opinion, the best.

In 2004, Philip Warren celebrated 25 years trading in Launceston, but the business itself is one of the oldest in Cornwall and, since it was established in 1880, had remained in one family, also farmer-butchers, until 1979. It is this adherence to high quality, providing a top-class service and working closely with local producers and meat processors, that has given this business the confidence to carry on despite the relentless progress of the supermarkets. It is also why customers return time and time again.

*Left:* Ray Gliddon in Philip Warren's cutting room.

Charles Gould is another farmer-butcher with an intense interest in producing good meat to high welfare and environmental standards, and, like the Lobb brothers, illustrates that the next generation of grazier-butchers is already showing its muscle. Zwartbles sheep and black pigs are the key animals on his farm near Ladock. The Zwartbles, originating from Holland, are the only commercial flock in Britain. These curiously attractive sheep, quite unlike any conventional British sheep breeds, produce dark, lean, tender and fine-grained meat that appeals to many of Cornwall's top chefs. From a farming point of view these animals are hardy, good mothers, docile and good converters, producing large, lean carcases with little wastage. Large Black pigs, also known as Cornish Blacks, are ideally suited to graze the farm. The Large Black is believed to have been introduced into Cornwall by trading ships returning from China. A rare breed of pig, the meat has a distinctive, 'proper pork' flavour. The lamb and pork are sold through his Truro shop, Fine Fettle Foods, where he also sells beef, poultry and venison raised by farmers following similarly sympathetic production systems. Like virtually all the farmer-grower-producers featured in this book, Charles Gould believes passionately in high-welfare, environmentally friendly farming systems: 'You can judge the quality of a farm by the diversity of the wildlife on it,' he said. Larkhill Farm has masses of skylarks and hares, and hedges and fields full of native wildflowers, herbs and grasses. 'If you care for the land, it will care for you.'

*Above:* Charles Gould.
*Below:* With his Cornish Black pigs.
*Right:* A Zwartbles sheep on Charles Gould 's farm.

# callenick farm beef fillet with lentils and crispy potatoes

This recipe comes from Hotel Tresanton, St Mawes, on the Roseland peninsula. The hotel, owned by Olga Polizzi, has been described as one of the most elegant in Britain. Head Chef Paul Wadham uses beef fillets supplied by Ralph Michell at Callenick Farm butchery, near Truro, and as much locally supplied fresh fish, shellfish and organic vegetables as he can. His unique style of cooking combines Mediterranean simplicity and flavours with English ingredients.

## ingredients

*Serves 4*

- 4 x 180 g Callenick Farm beef fillets, trimmed and ready to cook
- 4 large baking potatoes
- 20 organic baby carrots
- 100 g Puy lentils
- 1 carrot, finely diced
- 1/2 small onion, finely diced
- 1 rasher streaky bacon, diced
- 1 stick celery, finely diced
- bouquet garni
- 3 tbsp olive oil
- 1 tbsp balsamic vinegar (the best you can afford)
- 1 bunch flat-leaf parsley for garnish

## method

*Lentils:* Sweat the onion, celery and diced carrot, bacon and bouquet garni. Add lentils, and sweat a little longer.

Add 400 ml cold water, bring to the boil, and simmer until just cooked: this usually takes between 15 and 25 minutes.

When the lentils are cooked, discard the bouquet garni, spread the mixture on a tray, and sprinkle with the balsamic vinegar.

*Potatoes:* Wash and peel the baking potatoes and cut them into about 1 cm cubes. Bring the potato cubes to the boil in salted water, then remove from the heat and allow to cool naturally.

Heat a good frying-pan and add olive oil. Add the potatoes and allow them to colour until golden. Place on paper towel to remove excess oil, correct the seasoning and keep warm until required.

*Beef fillet:* Wash and peel the baby carrots, bring them to the boil in salted water, and simmer until just cooked. Strain and season.

Grill the seasoned beef fillet to medium rare: the timing depends on the thickness of the beef and the heat of your grill.

*To serve:* Reheat the lentil mixture in a saucepan with a little butter. Assemble the meal on a plate with the potatoes and carrots, garnishing with parsley.

*Top:* Paul Wadham.
*Above:* The terrace at Hotel Tresanton.

# 5 from the dairy

It is easy to imagine that Cornwall has always been a land of milk and honey, where dairy cattle have grazed lush, flower-filled meadows, for hundreds of years. West Cornwall is speckled with the brown and white shapes of Guernsey cows, while elsewhere the black and white Holstein Friesians dominate the landscape. Dairy farming is one of the county's biggest agricultural sectors, despite the poor financial returns for milk producers during the late 1990s and early part of the present century. It contributes significantly to the Cornish economy and was worth over £92 million in 2002. Most of the 115 million gallons of milk produced in Cornwall each year is sold direct to the large dairy processing companies, including Dairy Crest, at Davidstow near Camelford in North Cornwall.

The county's abundant grasslands and mild climate have made it renowned for its dairy products. Cornish clotted cream is the most famous, but ice cream and, more recently, Cornish cheeses have justly earned their reputation as high-quality foods. Yet in 1602, Richard Carew described much of the county as poorly suited to raising cattle:

> The middle part of the shire (saving the enclosures about some towns and villages) lieth waste and open, showeth a brackish colour, beneath heath and spiry grass, and serveth in a manner only to summer cattle.

The good grassland in the north of the county was rented by Devon and Somerset farmers for summer grazing. Milk from sheep and goats was mostly made into cheeses and butter, and little milk was drunk in its natural form: only the wealthy had copious quantities of cream and fresh milk, but did not drink milk in any quantity as it was thought to ferment in the stomach. Carew noted that until the

*Right:* Holstein Friesian cows at the Royal Cornwall Show.

Elizabethan era the common man's diet had been limited to whitsul – also known as the dairy white meats – in this case 'milk, sour milk, cheese, curds, butter, and such like as came from the cow and ewe.'

During the sixteenth and seventeenth centuries, cows replaced sheep and goats as the main milk animal, and butter and clotted cream (see panel below) became the best way of preserving surplus milk. These were easier to sell at market than fresh milk, which was always at risk of spoiling. Butter could be salted and packed into barrels for use in the lean winter months. Butter markets (in name, if

## clotted cream

Cornish clotted cream can only be called Cornish (as distinct from Devon or Somerset) if it is made in Cornwall from Cornish milk. It was awarded the EU's Protected Designation of Origin status in 1998, giving it the same protected status as other speciality regional food such as Parma ham, and Stilton and Parmesan cheeses. The best clotted cream is distinguished by its golden-yellow colour, silky texture and slightly nutty, creamy taste. Arguments still rage about how crusty the top of the cream should be, but the best should have a fine balance between a firm crust and smooth, thick cream beneath. Channel Island milk from Jersey and Guernsey cows, which has a high butterfat content, makes the best clotted cream. For hundreds of years almost every farm scalded surplus milk in the spring and summer to produce clotted cream and butter. The traditional method has hardly changed for centuries, although modern, large-scale production inevitably has brought short cuts and time-saving processes.

There are several theories about the evolution of clotting cream, including the influence of the Phoenicians who traded Middle Eastern spices, saffron and other foods in exchange for Cornish tin. Clotted cream is very similar to Turkish *kaymak*, a food found all over the Middle East, Afghanistan, Iran and even India. *Kaymak* is a rich, clotted cream, traditionally made from water-buffalo milk, in a similar way. This method for making Cornish clotted cream is taken from Edith Martin's *Cornish Recipes Ancient & Modern*, published by the Women's Institute in 1929:

Use new milk and strain at once, as soon as milked, into shallow pans. Allow it to stand for 24 hours in winter and 12 hours in summer. Then put the pan on the stove, or better still into a steamer containing water, and let it slowly heat until the cream begins to show a raised ring round the edge. When sufficiently cooked place in a cool dairy and leave for 12 or 24 hours. Great care must be taken in moving the pans so that the cream is not broken, both in putting on the fire and taking off. When required skim off the cream in layers into a glass dish for the table, taking care to have a good 'crust' on the top.

The ratio of milk to cream is 9:1, so this left plenty of whey to feed to pigs and calves.

Clotted cream, which has a minimum of 55 per cent butterfat, would have been served at tea time and with other sweet dishes for prosperous Cornish families, and some would have been churned into butter. This level of consumption of rich, fatty foods should be put in the context of a physically demanding lifestyle, where work was hard, hours were long and conditions often harsh. Cornish clotted cream has become a luxury food in our increasingly health-conscious society, yet is perhaps only 'bad' for us because of our modern, sedentary lifestyle. It is ironic that health-consciousness encourages many of us to drink skimmed milk, clotted cream's by-product.

*Above:* Taking his cows
to be milked, Mr Pethick
at Trevalga, near Boscastle.

not the actual buildings) are still to be found in Cornish towns such as Bodmin and
Redruth, and that of Helston is now part of the town's folk museum. By the end
of the sixteenth century the practice of clouting (clotting) cream was widespread
throughout the county: increasing numbers of homes had a heat source suitable
for gently heating milk for several hours to turn it into clotted cream. Celia Fiennes
enjoyed clotted cream in St Austell in 1698, and in 1775 the Revd William Gilpin,
visiting Cotehele in South East Cornwall, was also served a local cream tea: 'Here
we refreshed ourselves with tea, and larded our bread, after the fashion of the
county, with clouted cream.'

By the 1750s, the parish of Constantine had over 1,000 cows 'kept for milk'.
Dairy farming was increasing in southern and western parts of the county, where
the wealthier landowners were enclosing more land and establishing their own
dairy herds, depriving cottagers and farm-workers of the common land where
they would graze their house cows for much of the year. At the end of the
eighteenth century, dairying was a good way of earning a living, with the booming mining industry providing a ready local market. Farmers hired out cows to cow-
keepers – usually farm-workers and other labourers – who kept them for seven or
eight months and sold the milk, butter and cream in the most populated areas,
which in turn paid their rent. When the cow was ready to calve it was returned to

*Above:* Milking a Guernsey cow at the Royal Cornwall Show.

its owner and replaced by another, freshly calved animal. The agricultural historian G.B. Worgan noted in 1811 that there was also a profitable by-product – pigs:

> These cow-renters generally have a piece of ground allotted them by the farmer, on which they grow potatoes; with these, and with the scalded milk which has yielded cream for the butter, they fatten a great many young porkers.

Many cow-keepers used the higher moorland pastures during the summer. This was similar to the Welsh system of *hafod* – grazing cattle in the hills and uplands during the summer and returning them to lowland pasture and the home farm for the winter.

Ironically, it was the contraction of mining during the next 50 years that encouraged more Cornish farmers to switch from growing grain to producing milk. The completion of Brunel's bridge over the Tamar and the improvement in the railways made it possible to send fresh products from Cornwall to up-country markets for the first time. In 1875 the *West Briton* reported that dairy farming had expanded so rapidly in West Cornwall that six or seven tons of butter were being sent by train from Penzance each week:

The principal towns to which it is consigned are Dudley, Birmingham, Sheffield, Bristol and London... The present price of butter in Cornish markets is from 1s. to 1s. 1d. per lb. Six tons at this rate would realise £672. Fancy between £4,000 and £5,000 worth of fresh butter being sent away from one station in about one month! Large quantities are also sent away from Truro and other Cornish stations.

As the railways brought more tourists into the county, ice cream parlours sprang up (see Chapter 7), which, with cream teas, became a vital part of the new, but rapidly expanding, tourist trade. Although butter production had by now become mechanized, some smaller dairies and farms continued to make it by hand, rather than churning, until the middle of the twentieth century – hence the saying that a dairymaid's hands 'should be smooth as butter, white as milk, and cool as spring water.' By the end of the Victorian era, farmers and small dairies had set up milk rounds in the towns and villages. Fresh milk would be poured straight from the churn into the customer's jug or milk can. The first co-operative dairy processing companies were set up, making cream, butter, skimmed milk powder, and some cheese. These included Catchall Dairy near Sancreed and others at Wendron, Ludgvan, Trevarno and, later, St Erth and Lostwithiel. Milk was becoming big business.

The arrival of the Milk Marketing Board (MMB) in 1933 made it compulsory for all farmers to sell their milk to the board. The MMB fixed the price and marketed the milk, ostensibly to ensure a fairer return to farmers and balance the increasing power of the dairy processing companies. During the Second World War, grassland was ploughed up to grow potatoes and cereals, there was less milk, cream production stopped and butter was rationed. No doubt there were plenty of illicit pans of cream quietly heating on Cornish stoves during that time, making clotted cream and farmhouse butter even more of a treat to be enjoyed for its rarity. In 1942 a woman from Wadebridge was fined £3 for selling cream and butter. Her customers were also fined 10s. (50p) each.

Apart from Dairy Crest, A.E. Rodda & Son, and Newlands Farm (a company specializing in bottling only Cornish milk, and which has recently been bought by the dairy co-operative Milk Link), Cornwall has lost most of its large-scale milk processing facilities. As the British dairy industry becomes increasingly industrialized and homogenous, most Cornish milk leaves the county, destined for the anonymous national milk pool. It returns as butter, bottled milk, cheese, cream or dairy desserts, bringing no additional economic benefit to Cornish dairy farms. However, the demise of milk factories at St Erth, Lostwithiel and Camborne, which had inevitably absorbed most of the smaller dairies set up during the last 100 years, has created the opportunity for a growing number of milk producers to stamp their own identity on their milk by creating a niche range of rich, Cornish dairy products, none of them half as bad for you as the 'health police' would have you believe – providing you treat them with respect and consume them in moderation. Milk, cream, butter and cheese are made on a small scale, with great care, by men and women who use traditional methods and are passionate about their products. (See Chapter 6 for the story of the revival of Cornish cheese-making.)

Real milk has a layer of thick, golden cream that settles on the top: it tastes as milk should, and if you are looking for it, your first stop should be Barwick Farm, in an area delightfully named the Roseland. Nick and Barbara Michell are relative newcomers to processing. They started bottling their organic Jersey milk and making clotted cream and butter on their 80-acre, rented farm in 1999. Nick Michell's simple message is that 'unhomogenized, pasteurized milk tastes beautiful'. He is right. After separating the cream from the milk, butter and clotted cream are made using old-fashioned methods. The cream is heated slowly until it clots, then left to cool and rest before being potted the next day. Butter is still weighed, patted into blocks, and wrapped by hand. The quality speaks for itself, and the Michells' organic produce is in great demand, highly sought after by loyal customers, hotels and restaurants. They also sell full-cream, skimmed and semi-skimmed milk,

*Below and top right:*
Judging at the Royal
Cornwall Show.

as well as single and double cream. The modern, industrialized processes of homogenizing and heat-treating milk for bulk sales in supermarkets has created a characterless white water, with an unnaturally long shelf-life for such a perishable product. Most of the small dairy businesses in Cornwall bottling their own milk do not homogenize it, opting for a shorter shelf-life but knowing that the product has a far superior flavour. If stored in the correct conditions, most of this Cornish milk and cream should keep for up to a week. Names to look out for are Bradley's Dairy, Gwavas Jersey Farm, Trewithen Cornish Farm Dairy, and Jersey Cow Farm Foods. They all bottle milk and clot cream, and some make other dairy products, particularly yoghurt, crème fraîche, and smoothies, the newest Cornish dairy product, made from yoghurt and fruit purée at Helsett Farm, which is best known for ice cream.

The black and white Holstein Friesian cows have only become the breed of choice among milk producers in the last 40 years. Until the 1960s, Channel Island herds predominated in mid- and West Cornwall, while in North Cornwall, many farmers used the (then) dual-purpose Devon or South Devon cows, now kept specifically as beef animals. With the growing demand for higher yields, these were replaced first by Ayrshires and British Friesians, and then by the larger Holstein Friesians.

Barbara Lake, at Coads Green near Launceston, is another highly respected artisan producer who makes a limited quantity of clotted cream and butter each week, using milk from her nine Guernsey and Jersey cows. She still heats the milk on her Rayburn to yield the cream, but in common with other specialist producers, she keeps some elements of her craft a closely guarded secret.

The county's two biggest clotted cream producers are Trewithen Farm Foods, in the hands of Bill and Rachel Clarke, who produce dairy products following very high animal welfare and

*Below:* Nick Michell with his Jersey cows at Barwick Farm.

environmentally friendly farming principles, and Rodda's. A.E. Rodda & Son was the first company to commercialize clotted cream production and to devise a way of preserving the cream to give it a longer shelf-life. Like many other farmers' wives, Fanny Rodda made clotted cream in the traditional way and sold it to friends and neighbours. In the 1890s, she and her husband, Alfred, recognized that the growing tourist market was creating a rising demand for clotted cream to serve in cream teas for visitors. This in turn created a demand for the golden cream to take home, but it was not until 1924 that the techniques were perfected to make cream with the keeping qualities that allowed it to be sold outside the county. Demand continued to grow and soon Rodda's cream was on sale in prestigious London food halls such as Harrod's and Fortnum & Mason. It was only in the 1960s that the Rodda family gave up farming to concentrate on clotted cream production. Three generations are still actively involved in this family business, which buys milk from local farms and produces several tonnes of clotted cream each week. The company also makes crème frâiche, single and double cream and butter. Rodda's Cornish clotted cream is one of the best-known Cornish foods in the world, served on international airlines, in top hotels and restaurants, and sold in food halls and delicatessens all over Britain.

For some people, butter has become another forbidden fruit in the modern diet; but genuine Cornish butter, churned in Cornwall (unlike the infamous 'Cornish'

*Below:* Cows grazing near Trevalga on the north Cornish coast.

butter made in Somerset) is worth saving for feast days and special occasions. The golden-yellow blocks have a depth of flavour that most of us can only dream of, reflecting the grasses, flowers and herbs in the meadows grazed by Cornish cattle. Barwick Farm and Barbara Lake make butter using the sweet cream method, simply churning the cream until it thickens, extracting the buttermilk, and then shaping the pats by hand. 'We think the taste is a lot better making it this way,' Nick Michell said, reminding me that this was the way his father and grandfather made butter. Butter can also be made using a lactic fermentation method, where a culture is added to the cream to sour it before it is churned, and occasionally cheesemakers use leftover whey to make whey butter. Perhaps the most luxurious and rarest butter is clotted cream butter, occasionally made by Barbara Lake and a favourite of the late Queen Mother. Each has a distinctive flavour and texture – the choice is yours.

What is encouraging about these small-scale Cornish dairy businesses is that most developed to make the best use of their own milk, or have close links with dedicated Cornish suppliers, building relationships that underpin both farmer and manufacturer. The future for Cornish dairy farmers, and thus for the Cornish landscape, looks encouraging. Those who have opted for artisan dairy products, such as butter and cheese, have done better than those supplying the national commodity markets. Low prices and stand-offs with the supermarkets and milk processors meant that few of these producers made much money between 1997 and 2004.

Finally to a dairy sheep success story. Hugh Eddy is a young farmer who has diversified into making ewes milk yoghurt. He started milking sheep in 2001, but it was not until 2003 that he decided to make yoghurt. After months of experimenting with the recipe in his mother's kitchen, he started selling natural ewes milk yoghurt at local farmers' markets that summer. 'We must have made 100 batches, but we learnt the techniques needed to get the right product,' he said. Just one year later he was winning prizes at the Royal Cornwall Show and in the prestigious Taste of the West regional food and drink awards. Davas Farm yoghurts have limited availability, mostly at farmers' markets and in selected retail outlets. Although Hugh Eddy's 70 ewes are a small-scale operation, this is a business with potential, driven by a determined, hard-working, and enthusiastic young farmer.

*Top:* Rodda's Cornish clotted cream.
*Above:* Hugh Eddy winning Best New Product award at the Royal Cornwall Show, 2004.

# cornish cream tea

As Cornwall's most famous food, clotted cream is the essence of the traditional Cornish cream tea. It also features as a key ingredient in hotel and restaurant kitchens across the county: the five million people who visit Cornwall and the Isles of Scilly each year would be disappointed not to be offered clotted cream as the natural accompaniment to many sweet dishes.

There is a long-running debate between the traditionalists and the rest as to whether a traditional cream tea should use scones or splits (see Chapter 10). Scones seem to win on the grounds of convenience, but splits (or tuffs, as they are called in parts of the county), are deemed to be correct. Splits served with clotted cream and treacle are known as Thunder and Lightning. Equally important is the order in which cream and jam are applied. In Cornwall, it is jam followed by cream; cross the River Tamar and the order is reversed. Woe betide anyone serving them the wrong way round on either side of the county border! A Cornish clotted cream producer's wife once committed this sin when helping with teas at a cricket match – it was three years before she was allowed to help again.

There are numerous variations on what constitutes a proper Cornish cream tea, but they appear to follow roughly the same rules.

*Above:* A Cornish cream tea served in the garden, courtesy of Trewithen Cornish Farm Dairy and Boddingtons (see page 162).

## ingredients

*Serves any number*

- at least one split (or scone) per person
- a large bowl of Cornish clotted cream
- Cornish jam – try Boddington's strawberry conserve, preserves from Cornish Country Meadows, or Carnon Valley conserves
- a large pot of tea

## method

Halve the splits or scones and spread them with jam, followed by a generous serving of clotted cream. Some recipes suggest dusting the splits with icing sugar, but this seems to be gilding the lily. A bowl of Cornish strawberries or raspberries makes a pleasant addition. Enjoy – then go for a long walk.

# 6 taste the terroir

Mention cheese and Cornwall in the same sentence and most people respond 'Cornish Yarg'. Yarg is without doubt the best-known handmade Cornish cheese, but, unlike other British provincial cheeses such as Wensleydale and Cheshire, Cornish Yarg has a short history, stretching back some 20 years rather than eight or nine centuries. It is named after Alan and Jenny Gray – 'Yarg' is 'Gray' reversed – who started making the cheese in the early 1980s. They were unable to expand production sufficiently to keep up with demand, but fortunately for Cornish cheese-making, were put in touch with Michael and Margaret Horrell, who were looking for ways to diversify their dairy farm. The Grays started making cheese for the Horrells, and eventually sold them the recipe and retired. Within a year of the Horrells starting cheese production on a small scale, Cornish Yarg had gained national recognition due to the quality of the cheese and its unique nettle coating. At that time there was a strong interest in the revival of traditional cheese-making skills, and Yarg, although a new speciality cheese, hit the mark. It is made on two farms, one near Liskeard, the other near Penryn, using milk from both farms.

The cheese is made in open vats, where the curds are cut by hand to release the whey. The curds are then milled and pressed in moulds overnight before being placed in brine baths for salting. Once the cheeses have been coated in nettles (which are picked and frozen for year-round use) they are left to mature in the ripening room where they are turned daily. Yarg is a semi-hard, full-fat, cows milk cheese, made to be eaten young. It is slightly acidic and crumbly, similar to, but slightly firmer than, a Wensleydale or Cheshire cheese. The distinctive nettle coating, which gives the cheese a green-grey, edible rind, has caught the public's imagination, and while the Lynher Dairies Cheese Company makes several other cheeses, Cornish Yarg remains the best-known artisan Cornish cheese.

*Right:* Cornish cheeses – Yarg, Cornish Blue, Trelawny, Gevrik and St Keverne Square, at The Cheese Shop, Truro.

Although Yarg is a thoroughly modern cheese, it has strong historic antecedents. The seventeenth-century writer Gervase Markham considered that a new milk, nettle cheese, in this case ripened on nettles, was 'the finest of all summer cheeses which can be eaten.' Today, with dairy farming more significant in Cornwall than in many other English counties, Cornish cheeses are among some of the most vibrant and innovative in Britain. In the late 1980s, when the great cheese connoisseur Patrick Rance revised his seminal work on British cheese, *The Great British Cheese Book*, six Cornish cheeses were made on two farms. In 2004 there were almost 60 artisan Cornish cheeses made on a handful of farms, with more in development. Since 1988, more than 450 new British cheeses have appeared. The rapid renaissance of Cornish cheese-making combines traditional methods with old and new recipes, even if it no longer takes place in farmhouse kitchens – modern food safety legislation requires acres of stainless steel and white walls. While some cheeses are made on a larger scale than others, many are winning awards in national and international competitions, and Cornish cheeses have become a major part of the new Cornish food scene.

Looking at the range of cheeses available in delicatessens and specialist shops, both English and Continental, it is hard to believe that until recently there was no long-established tradition of distinctive, indigenous cheeses on the Cornish side of the River Tamar. One of the reasons for this was the late development of the Cornish dairy sector: until the end of the eighteenth century, agriculture played second fiddle to the county's real wealth-generator, mining. This is not to say that the early Bronze Age farmers did not make cheese; only that, until the early 1980s, Cornish cheese-making was not a significant commercial activity. The success of Cornish cheese is a modern phenomenon.

Making Cornish Yarg.
*Left:* Filling moulds with milled curds.
*Below:* Cheese moulds.
*Bottom:* Coating a cheese with nettles.

More than 3,000 years ago, the early Celts settling in Cornwall (and elsewhere) discovered that during hot weather milk stored in pottery or leather containers quickly soured and separated into curds and whey, making soft, curdy cheeses. The next advance was understanding that animal rennet, found in the stomachs of young calves, coagulates milk and makes the curds form faster. Rennet

produces a different fermentation process from ordinary souring and also con- tains enzymes that work on the cheese over a prolonged period, helping it to ripen and develop flavour, and making a harder type of cheese that keeps longer. Alternatives to rennet were plant juices, such as those from milk thistle or butter- wort. Most modern renneted cheeses use artificial, vegetarian rennets. The next step was discovering that by pressing out most of the whey and rubbing salt into the outside of the cheese a rind would form, and the keeping qualities improved. The Celts probably even smoked some cheeses – they were already smoking meat and fish to preserve them. This technique has been revived by Nigel Ekins at Cornish Cuisine, whose Tesyn – a button goats milk cheese – won the best new cheese World Cheese Awards in 2002. By the time the Romans invaded Britain, a well-developed cheese culture was in place, and when they arrived at the River Tamar Cornish cheeses would have been either soft, curd cheeses or hard, semi-pressed cheeses, most likely made from goats or ewes milk.

In medieval times the young, soft, curd cheeses were often known as 'green' cheeses, not because of their colour but because they were placed on mats of nettle leaves to drain, acquiring the name of nettle cheeses – the forerunners of Cornish Yarg, perhaps? Cheese-making remained small scale, for local use only. Given that, with the exception of the wealthy, the Cornish diet was so poor that cheese would barely feature in it, it is not surprising that one seventeenth-century traveller noted that 'there were not many cheeses to be found in the whole of that county and what there was, was very bad.' Certainly Cornwall missed out on the cheese boom that took place elsewhere in Britain in the seventeenth century, which confirmed the status and development of England's great provincial cheeses, Stilton and Cheddar.

However, as dairy farming expanded and became more sophisticated in the eighteenth century, cheese- making provided a use for the glut of spring and summer milk: made into cheese it could be preserved for the winter. The social historian A.K. Hamilton Jenkin believed that, during the eighteenth and nineteenth

## pasteurized or unpasteurized farmhouse cheeses?

Many cheese experts claim that the finest cheeses are those made from unpasteurized milk, which gives the cheese a unique flavour and aroma. Sadly, the milk used to make most cheeses is pasteurized. In cheese dairies where the milk is bought in rather than used straight from the farm, pasteurization ensures that any potentially harmful bacteria have been dealt with. Some cheesemakers argue that pasteurized milk gives a more consistent product, but the downside is that, as with many other foods, we are in danger of over-sanitizing our entire food chain to the detriment of the food itself. The **Slow Food** move- ment is doing its best to protect the few remaining raw-milk (unpasteur- ized) cheeses, but as each year passes it becomes more apparent that the growing army of health officials who wish to monitor all we eat and drink will continue to find every reason they can to end centuries of cheese- making tradition, leaving us with dull and uninspiring foods. Be careful about the word 'farmhouse' when used to describe cheese: it does not necessarily mean that the cheese is handmade on a farm in small batches, or by using artisan methods.

centuries, many of the cow-keepers would have followed the ancient pastoral system of *hafod*, the Welsh word for summer quarters:

*Above:* Nigel Ekins smoking cheeses at Cornish Cuisine.

> The herdsmen would leave the *gwavas* or winter homestead and proceed into the high-country moorlands which, although too exposed for permanent settlement, yielded sufficiently good pasture for the flocks during a few months of the year. In these summer quarters dairy-work would form the chief occupation. Hence the Cornish word *laity* or milk-house may be considered to have had much the same meaning as the Welsh *haffoty* or summer-house. With the fall of the year the herds-men would leave their summer pastures and return once more to the shelter of the *gwavas* or *hendra* (old homestead).

At this time of year, and just after calving, the cows would be at their most productive, so much of the dairy work would take place *in situ*, just as summer cheeses are still made in the mountain pastures of France, Spain and Switzerland. Traditionally, it would have been the only way to preserve the milk. There is plenty of evidence to indicate that this summer grazing system continued for over a century. The *West Briton* of 29 April 1869 advertised, 'At Sibly Back, in the parish of St Cleer, Good Summering for cattle, at 6s. [30p] and 10s. [50p] per head.' However, other reports suggest that the cow-keepers made more money from selling milk, cream and butter than cheese.

By the early 1800s the Royal Cornwall Agricultural Society was holding dairy classes at the Royal Cornwall Show, to encourage more cheese-making. As local dairy processing companies emerged, the principal products seemed to be butter and clotted cream. Why? One reason may be that at the time most Cornish cattle were Channel Island types, producing rich, high-fat milk, ideal for butter and cream, less suited for cheese, which requires lower fat and higher protein levels. However, once pasteurized milk was introduced in the 1890s, some cheese manufacturing did take place (see panel on page 88), as pasteurization eliminated the risk from larger-scale cheese-making. Small-scale, domestic production continued for personal and local use. The county council worked hard in the first half of the twentieth century to encourage rural women to learn or improve their dairy skills, and the county started to get a reputation for its dairy produce. In November 1923, the *West Briton* reported great success at the London Dairy Show:

*Below:* Sue Proudfoot's Trelawny cheeses.

The county obtained six first prizes, six second, five third, four fourth and three fifth, beside securing the second and reserve for the shield in the inter-county cheese-making competition.

Sadly, the paper did not give details of what the cheese was, and it seems that these Cornish cheeses did not achieve a lasting national reputation.

During the Second World War any specific Cornish cheeses lost their identity when almost all traditional and local cheese-making stopped. Throughout Britain only two cheeses were officially made on a factory scale: Cheddar and Wensleydale. In the early 1950s, after rationing ended, it was clear that the Milk Marketing Board was supremely disinterested in encouraging any revival of traditional or artisan cheeses. In 1984, the new milk quotas delivered the final, near-fatal blow to English cheese-making. Introduced to deal with the European 'milk lake', quotas forced all dairy farmers to reduce milk production by 7 per cent. There was no political will to sustain any incentives for specialist cheesemakers, even though they were a tiny part of the dairy industry, using less than 0.5 per cent of Britain's total annual production.

*Above:* Sue Proudfoot's Keltic Gold.

We are lucky that a few farmers with a long history of making cheeses doggedly persisted, and were finally rewarded by the encouragement of figures such as the late Patrick Rance and Randolph Hodgson. In the late 1970s and 1980s Patrick Rance campaigned for the renaissance of British cheese-making. His work with artisan cheesemakers and his one-man onslaught against the movement for cheap, mass-produced, pre-packed, creamery cheese has been continued by Randolph Hodgson, founder of the Neal's Yard Dairy. Rance knew that the manufacturers' and the Milk Marketing Board's insistence that there was no difference between factory and genuine handmade cheeses was nonsense. Anyone doing a taste comparison between block Cheddar and a genuine handmade Cheddar instantly recognizes that this is not so. What the manufacturers and supermarkets omitted to say was that mass-produced, block cheeses were a far more convenient way of selling cheese than having to cut and wrap each order individually, and – as a secondary issue – needing the knowledge to care for cheeses properly.

Fortunately for Cornwall, soon after the Horrells developed Cornish Yarg, Caryl and John Minson arrived at Menallack in West Cornwall. Although in 2004 they

were threatening to retire, the Minsons are so passionate about cheese that they cannot bear to give up. Working in small batches, they make the biggest range of Cornish cheese types and styles.

In a different league altogether is the cheese made by Dairy Crest at Davidstow, in North Cornwall. Set up in 1951 by Cow and Gate, this is Britain's largest, most modern and high-tech, fully automated cheese-making plant. Upgraded and re-equipped in 2004, it has the capacity to produce up to 1,000 tonnes of cheese a week. Two of Britain's most popular and successful mature cheddar cheeses are made here, Davidstow and Cathedral City, both widely available in most supermarkets. When cheese production started at Davidstow in 1951 the milk was collected in churns from nearby farms, most producing no more than ten gallons a day. Today milk is supplied direct from 300 farms in Cornwall and Devon, all within a 50-mile radius.

Although 90 per cent of the cheese sold in Britain is creamery – i.e. factory – made, one of the advantages of not having a long-established history of indigenous cheeses is that most Cornish cheeses are genuine artisan cheeses, handmade in small quantities, often on the farms where the milk is produced. Despite hygiene laws requiring squeaky clean, ultra-sanitized dairies, dominated by stainless steel, white coats and boots, and blue hairnets, low-tech, high quality, artisan cheese-making continues to create products with a depth of flavour that reflects the Cornish countryside.

One of the joys of the large, growing, range of speciality Cornish cheeses is that many change according to the season, the grasses the cattle graze on, and the minerals in the ground. Some even vary according to whether the milk is from the evening or morning milking. Much too depends on the individual cheesemaker's skills: two cheesemakers using identical milk in identical conditions, then maturing the cheese in the same way produce two quite different products. A good cheese is consistent in appearance, texture and overall flavour, but these other subtleties and changes turn cheese-making into a culinary art form.

The range of Cornish cheeses is astonishing (see list on page 94) – from white-rinded brie styles, to soft, fresh goats milk cheeses; young, semi-hard, and rind-washed cheeses, to Cornish Blue, all made to be eaten young. Stephen Gunn, Cornwall's only cheesemonger, believes that, like fine wines, the best cheeses reflect the *terroir* in which they are produced, the soil type, the climate, and the terrain all having an influence on the final flavour and texture of the cheese. Cornish cheesemakers are fortunate that Stephen spotted a need for an *affineur* in Cornwall. He brings knowledge, enthusiasm and passion to the Cornish cheese scene, contributing to it by working with cheesemakers to develop new cheeses and by buying young cheeses, allowing their full potential to develop and mature in his cheese cellars.

*Left top and middle:* The Cheese Shop, Truro.
*Bottom left:* Philip Stansfield and his Cornish Blue cheeses.
*Above:* Stephen Gunn, Cornwall's only cheese-monger.

## cornish cheeses by maker

*Note:* all cheeses use cows milk unless stated otherwise.

### Cornish Cheese Co.

Beast of Bodmin – soft, white-rinded (i.e. mould ripened), rind washed

Cornish Blue – semi-hard, blue

Cornish Camembert – soft, white-rinded

Farmhouse Cornish Brie – soft, white-rinded

### Cornish Country Larder

Chatel – soft, white-rinded

Cornish Organic Brie – soft, white-rinded

Cornish Smokey – semi-hard, smoked

Gevrik – soft, white-rinded, goats milk

St Anthony – soft, white-rinded, goats milk

St Endellion – soft, white-rinded

Westcountry Cornish Brie – soft, white-rinded

### Cornish Cuisine

Cornish Smoked Cheddar

St Agnes Brie – soft, white-rinded

Tesyn – smoked, soft, goats milk

Tintagel Organic – smoked cheddar

Tresco – smoked, hard, goats milk

Trevellas – smoked blue

### Cornish Farmhouse Cheeses

Buffalo Soft – fresh, soft, buffalo milk

Cheetham's Chough – semi-hard, ewes milk

Cornish Feta – feta cubes in oil, goats milk

Cornish Herb Whirl – soft, fresh, with herbs, goats milk

Cornish Smoke – semi-hard

Fingals – soft, fresh

Garden of Eden – semi-hard, with herbs and sun-dried tomatoes

Heligan – semi-soft, with lemon, ewes and cows milk

Menallack Farmhouse – semi-hard

Menallack Chives and Garlic – semi-hard, with chives and garlic

Mrs Finn – semi-soft, ewes and cows milk

Nanterrow – semi-soft, ewes milk

Nanterrow with chives and garlic – semi-soft, ewes milk

Polmesk – soft, fresh, flavour added, goats milk

St Erme – semi-hard, with chillies

St Laudus – semi-hard, blued after maturing

St Piran – semi-soft with saffron, ewes and cows milk

Tala – semi-hard, ewes milk

Treverva Green – semi-soft, with green peppercorns, ewes and cows milk

Vintage Farmhouse – semi-hard

Vithen – soft, white, fresh, goats milk

### Dairy Crest at Davidstow

Cathedral City – hard, cheddar

Davidstow – hard, cheddar

### Lynher Dairies Cheese Company

Cornish Black Pepper – soft, fresh, with black pepper

Cornish Garland – semi-hard, with oregano, thyme and spring onion

Cornish Herb and Garlic – soft, fresh, with mixed herbs and garlic

Cornish Tarragon – soft, fresh, with tarragon

Cornish Tiskey – semi-hard, with herbs and sun-dried tomatoes

Cornish Wild Garlic Yarg – semi-hard, wrapped in wild garlic leaves

Cornish Yarg – semi-hard, wrapped in nettles

Stithians Special – semi-hard

### Neet Foods

St Marwenne – soft cheese balls in oil

St Marwenne – soft cheese balls in oil, goats milk

### Toppenrose Dairy

St Keverne Square – soft, white-rinded, square

Toppenrose Gold – soft, white-rinded, added Jersey cream

Trenance Softie – fresh cream cheese

### Whalesborough Farm Foods

Cornish Herbert – soft, fresh

Keltic Gold – semi-hard, rind-washed

Miss Muffet – semi-hard, washed curds

Trelawny – semi-hard

### Sue Williams

Carn Brea – soft, fresh, goats milk

Carn Brea with chives – soft, fresh, with chives, goats milk

Carn Brea with herbs – soft, fresh, with thyme and sage, goats milk

One Cornish cheese that sums up this relationship with the *terroir* is Cornish Blue. Made in the shadow of a pile of granite stones and rocks known as the Cheesewring, which perches on the edge of Bodmin Moor (see photo on page 12), Philip and Carol Stansfield's cheese depends on the clean air, rich pastures, and the unique microclimate of that part of South East Cornwall to produce the milk that is made into Cornwall's only blue cheese. Careful production and maturing create a soft blue cheese, similar to Gorgonzola, made to be eaten young. Production started in 2001, after two years of painstaking research and trial cheese-making, but already this Cornish cheese is in steady demand at farmers' markets, in supermarkets and fine food shops.

*Top:* Making Cornish Blue, on the edge of Bodmin Moor.
*Above:* Sue Proudfoot – a genuine artisan cheese-maker.

The new generation of Cornish cheesemakers have no links to any traditional cheeses and nor do they come from families with a history of making cheese on any significant commercial scale. Sue Proudfoot, at Marhamchurch, not far from the north Cornish coast, started making cheese in 1999 using milk from her farm's dairy herd. A genuine artisan cheesemaker, she makes limited quantities of cheese, and although the business is growing, it is strictly on her terms: she refuses to compromise her high standards in order to increase production. Sue started with improvised equipment and a basic cheese-making course at a local agricultural college. She is passionate about her craft, and understands the complexities of small-scale, artisan cheese-making. 'It is not a button pushing exercise,' she said. Her dedication has paid off: among her satisfied customers are the food hall at Fortnum & Mason, Paxton & Whitfield, and many small delicatessens and specialist shops. Although there are no longer dairy cows at Whalesborough Farm, Sue buys her milk from a local, dedicated herd of organic Ayrshires, guaranteeing year-round consistency. As long as cheesemakers like Sue Proudfoot and Caryl Minson continue these relationships, and enterprises such as Lynher Dairies and the Cornish Cheese Company keep milking their cows to supply their own cheese dairies, Cornish cheese-making will build on good foundations.

# cornish early potato, asparagus and yarg salad

This recipe combines Cornish Yarg with two seasonal delicacies grown in Cornwall – asparagus and early potatoes. It was devised by Mike Maguire, from Trengilly Wartha near Helston, as part of a promotional campaign for Cornish Early new potatoes. It reflects the contemporary style of cooking that Mike uses with great success at the widely acclaimed gastropub, which has won numerous awards.

## ingredients

*Serves 4*

For the salad

- 400 g Cornish Early potatoes
- 2 bundles thin asparagus spears
- 100 g Cornish Yarg
- 100 g mixed baby salad leaves and herbs

For the dressing

- 1 tbsp white wine vinegar
- 2 tbsps virgin olive oil
- 1 tbsp sunflower oil
- 1 tsp grain mustard
- 1 tsp Cornish honey

*Above:* Mike Maguire.
*Left:* Recipe prepared for *Gourmet Cornwall* by Gerry Boriosi and Emma Hoskins at Cornwall College.

## method

Rub the potatoes under running water to remove any flaky skin. Bring them to the boil in cold, lightly salted water and cook them until they are yielding but still firm. Drain and leave to stand, covered with a cloth.

Whisk together the ingredients for the dressing, or put them all in a jam jar and shake it vigorously. Pour the resulting vinaigrette into a bowl.

Dice or slice the warm potatoes and toss them in the vinaigrette. The potatoes will absorb the flavours better when warm.

Trim the hard stalks of the asparagus. If the spears are too long, snap them in two. Plunge them into lightly salted boiling water and cook for a couple of minutes. When cooked, the spears should yield but still have some bite. Refresh them immediately in iced water and, while still just warm, drain and add to the potatoes, along with the salad leaves and herbs.

Divide the salad between four plates and, using a vegetable peeler, cut thin strips of Cornish Yarg to put on top of each salad.

# 7 frozen delights

For most people, a visit to the seaside is not complete without at least one ice cream, and if the queue outside Jelberts in Newlyn is anything to go by, the art of real ice cream making is alive and well in Cornwall. At the height of the summer season it is impossible to walk through any Cornish town, harbour village or seaside resort without being assailed by a range of ice cream products. Yet there is a world of difference between the simple process that Jim Glover of Jelberts uses for his ice cream, and the mass-produced product consisting of air, more air, emulsifiers, stabilizers, sugar, vegetable fat, dextrose, glycerine and the occasional nod in the direction of dairy produce that is churned out of factories by the millions of litres each year. That, to me, seems more like a chemistry experiment than a high-class food.

A relatively new item in the Cornish food lexicon, ice cream in a form we would recognize has been made in Britain for just over 300 years. It first made a grand entrance in 1671 at the court of King Charles II, who was keen to introduce Continental fashions on his return to London from exile in France. The first published ice cream recipe was, by all accounts, in *Mrs Eale's Receipts*, in 1718. The earliest of these sensational iced confections would have been nothing more than frozen cream, sugar and flavourings but, in the mid-eighteenth century, adding eggs to the recipe led to smoother, custard-based ices on which modern ice creams are based.

By the second half of the eighteenth century, ice creams were being made in elaborate moulds and shapes, with a range of extraordinary and innovative flavours, showing that many of what we think of as new and novel modern flavours have strong historical roots. Recipes recorded from that period include pistachio, jasmine, white coffee, burnt filbert cream ice and parmesan cream ice. Just as exotic

*Right:* Roskilly's ice cream at the Royal Cornwall Show.

fruit and vegetables became one of the benchmarks of competition between grand houses in the nineteenth century, so in the eighteenth century status was measured by elaborate desserts, including the fashionable new iced cream.

Ice cream was probably first enjoyed by Cornwall's grand houses in the eighteenth century, as the fashion spread out from London, and the invention of the ice-house made ice available on demand for cooling drinks (but not for consumption), and for chilled puddings including ice creams. By the end of that century, many of the grandest Cornish families and estates had built, or were in the process of constructing, ice-houses. These included the Rashleigh estate at Fowey, Pencarrow House near Wadebridge and Mount Edgcumbe, overlooking the River Tamar. The need was probably as much to do with social prestige as with following culinary trends.

Building and filling ice-houses was a massive exercise, and it is easy to imagine large numbers of servants being dispatched to cut, move and stack the ice whenever a cold snap settled in. The ice usually came from frozen rivers, flooded fields, specially constructed ponds or, as in the case of Polkyth House, near St Austell, from the bottom of the china-clay pits at Hensbarrow. Once packed and covered with straw, it could remain frozen for up to two years, although it is likely that Cornwall's mild climate might have restricted consistent ice supplies. In 1811, for example, the winter was damp and mild, and G.B. Worgan noted that it was 'no place for skaters' and 'the gentlemen's ice-houses were seldom filled'.

The first commercial cargoes of Norwegian ice arrived in London in 1815 or 1816, and were later supplemented by ice from Greenland and the USA. By the 1870s, Norwegian ice was arriving in Penzance in regular quantities, even though Cornwall had its own ice works by then, mainly to supply the thriving fishing industry. The Gulval ice works were probably set up in 1860–70, and soon had stores in Newlyn and St Ives; another was built at Dozmary Pool near Altarnun, in 1889, providing ice for fish sent from Looe to London. Imported ice was also used by commercial confectioners for ice cream making, and in private homes. Once the railway link between Cornwall and the rest of England had been completed, large quantities of ice were easily obtainable from commercial companies, for example in Plymouth (where it was imported from America) or in Penzance, making many ice-houses redundant. For a house such as Lanhydrock, near Bodmin, which was close to the new railway, it was simpler to have ice delivered by train from Plymouth each day, to be collected by pony and trap from the station.

Ice cream did not remain a luxury food for long. The combination of commercially available ice and new machinery meant that from the mid-nineteenth century it could be manufactured on a far greater scale. The influx of Italians, with a long tradition of ice cream making, into London and other major cities influenced its development too. Suddenly ice cream entered the mass market. Everyone could afford a hokey pokey – a two- or three-coloured neapolitan ice cream, cut into small squares or slices, the name probably a corruption of *Gelati! Ecco un poco* – or a penny lick, which was a small portion of ice cream sold in a reuseable dish. (Nowadays, ice cream is such a favourite that we each consume an average of eight litres of the stuff a year. The British ice cream market is worth £1 billion annually but we are, apparently, only bit-part players compared with the Americans, Danes, Austrialians and New Zealanders who lead the ice cream consumption league table.)

For Cornwall, with growing dairy and tourism industries, ice cream was an obvious product to develop, but it remained highly seasonal until the 1920s when modern continuous freezing techniques were introduced. As ice cream became popular and affordable, ice cream parlours sprang up all over the country, and although ice cream was and still is an essential part of the tourist experience, most of these ice cream parlours have either disappeared or now sell more than just ice cream. Frozen delights of varying quality are sold next to Cornish pasties, newspapers or groceries. Harts in St Ives, for example, for many years one of the best-known ice cream parlours, is no longer, and its building is now part of a national burger chain.

Treleaven's is a notable exception. One of the new kids on the ice cream block, it has three ice cream parlours – in Looe, Tintagel and Polperro – selling a range of luxury Cornish ice creams and sorbets, all handmade in small batches using as much local produce as possible. 'Milk and cream are about 90 per cent of the ingredients, and they are all Cornish,' explained Andrew Treleaven, adding that he

*Left:* Jelbert's vanilla ice cream, served in a cone, or with clotted cream and a chocolate flake.

*Above:* Jim Glover
of Jelberts, Newlyn.

knows the exact provenance of these ingredients. His nationally award-winning ice creams, in 36 flavours ranging from vanilla to banoffi, and orange and mascarpone, are made to exacting Italian artisan principles. He also makes ice creams and sorbets to order for local restaurants and hotels.

Two of the oldest Cornish manufacturers still in business are Jelberts and Kellys. Kellys was set up over 100 years ago, and is still owned by the same family, making a range of ice creams using local milk and clotted cream. In addition to supplying its own shops and fleet of vans, the company sells through other retail and catering outlets in Cornwall.

In contrast, Jelberts has resisted the temptation to expand and remains a one-off, niche product, probably the nearest thing to homemade ice cream that you can buy in Cornwall. Based in Newlyn, it grew out of a dairy business run by Jim Glover's grandfather before the Second World War, which delivered local milk and other dairy products in and around the town. Although it is not clear exactly when Jelberts started making ice cream, it was probably after the war, when milk and cream rationing ended, that it became a serious part of the business. Still made from the closely guarded, secret recipe used by Jim Glover's uncle and grandfather, small batches of ice cream are produced each day according to demand. No preservatives or additives, no e-numbers or anything else artificial – just pure dairy goodness in a tub or cone. Jelberts' only product is vanilla ice cream, which you can adulterate with a chocolate flake if you must, or top with a dollop of golden Cornish clotted cream, which is how most people eat it. This may seem a little like gilding the lily, as the ice cream is so good that it needs no dressing up to improve its clean flavour and slightly soft, whipped texture.

Jim Glover explained that his product is made to be eaten fresh – if put in a freezer for any time it becomes so rock-hard that it is difficult to serve. Believe it or not, that is a good thing, as it indicates the low level of overrun – the technical term for air, which is what bulks out most ice creams, creating the smooth, light texture that is typical of modern ice cream. Denser, harder, granular textures signal that you are eating the real thing without all the added 'extras' that do little except add more profit to their manufacturers' pockets. Described by one fan as 'heaven in a tub', relish Jelberts' ice cream while you can: Jim Glover may be the last generation to run this business.

Jelberts' original shop in Newlyn, which was also once a tearoom, is open only from April until the end of October. It would be easy to miss these understated premises on New Road, but for locals and those in the know this is the only place to go for old-fashioned, proper dairy ice cream. The recipe may be virtually unchanged for more than 50 years, but technology has made the process simpler. Jim Glover remembers churning the mixture by hand in a wooden tub filled with ice; now stainless steel paddles churn it automatically. Nevertheless, this remains a simple, one-man operation. Although this is quintessentially a craft product, like all other modern ice cream makers, and indeed all speciality food producers, Jelberts has been unable to avoid the raft of food hygiene regulations that have created a manufacturing environment that can only be described as a monument to stainless steel, white coats, hairnets and ultra-sanitized conditions.

   Undoubtedly war-time rationing was the start of the adulteration of pure dairy ice cream recipes, as cream and eggs were unavailable, and manufacturers found that vegetable oils made a good substitute. So much so that today the very cheapest mass-produced versions have little if any dairy content at all. Unlike the USA and many EU countries, Britain allows ice cream manufacturers to produce something that can contain up to 50 per cent air, or overrun, when measured in volume, and that can be made using non-dairy fat or vegetable oils. Although any product calling itself *dairy* ice cream must contain dairy produce, the existence of the non-dairy product does nothing to support Britain's dairy farmers. Which brings us back to Cornwall and the strong links between small, specialist ice cream makers and Cornish milk production.

*Below:* Jelberts, Newlyn.

Clotted Cream
Vanilla
Hokey Pokey

Triple Chocolate

Strawberry

- Passion Fruit
  Sorbet
- Blackcurrant
  Yoghurt

- Lemon

- Rum + Raisin

*Above and right:*
Roskilly's ice cream at the
Royal Cornwall Show.
*Pages 106–7:* Helsett Farm
Ice Cream organic ice
cream, made with Cornish
clotted cream and egg
yolks, by Sarah Talbot-
Ponsonby and Elia Allen.

The good news is that in the last 20 years a handful of enterprising Cornish dairy farmers have started making top-quality ice cream. Don't be confused by the words 'premium', 'luxury' or 'super premium', as these too have been taken over by the mass manufacturers in a scenario that is probably somewhere between the child's paradise of the Willy Wonka Chocolate Factory and the adult nightmare of the Sorcerer's Apprentice. These farmers recognized that a 'back to basics' approach was needed, using high-quality ingredients – their own milk, cream and eggs – to make something as close to home-made ice creams as possible, a craft product with a depth of flavour and a clear taste that bears no relation to the mass-produced version.

Tregellast Barton sits towards the end of the Lizard peninsula in picturesque St Keverne. Pretty it may be, but as long ago as the mid-1980s, faced with a number of issues including the new milk quota system, the Roskilly family realized that the future lay in making more money from their own milk. Ice cream production began in earnest in 1989. The 170-acre farm has been fully organic since 1996, and uses its own organic jersey milk and cream for Roskilly's ice cream, plus a wide variety of flavours, most prepared on the farm. The philosophy according to Philip Tanswell of Roskilly's, is to 'make the best possible products, using the best possible ingredients'. Up to 45 flavours of ice cream, frozen yoghurt and sorbet are available, either sold direct from the farm in its Croust House tearooms, or at shows and events, and in outlets across Cornwall and the South West.

Drive up the North Cornwall coast and the landscape is dominated by pastureland grazed by dairy cows (see photo on page 80), and some cereal growing. It is a reminder of why this part of Cornwall is so well suited to grass and milk production. Not far from Boscastle is Helsett Farm Ice Cream, described as a small, mother and daughter-run operation that produces homemade, old-fashioned ice cream. It is, and it is more than just that. Sarah Talbot-Ponsonby started making ice cream on the farm in 1985 in a response to the crisis caused by the introduction of the EU milk quotas, which limited the amount of milk each dairy farmer could produce and sell, but fortunately from which ice cream production was notably absent. Many despairing milk producers, in Cornwall and elsewhere, saw this as their salvation. Helsett Farm, Callestick Farm (near Truro) and Roskillys were among those who set up as a direct result of that intervention.

The Helsett Farm cows are pedigree Ayrshires, producing a golden, slightly creamy, organic milk, some of which goes into the ice cream, some to Sue Proudfoot in nearby Marhamchurch for cheese-making (see Chapter 6), and some into other dairy products.

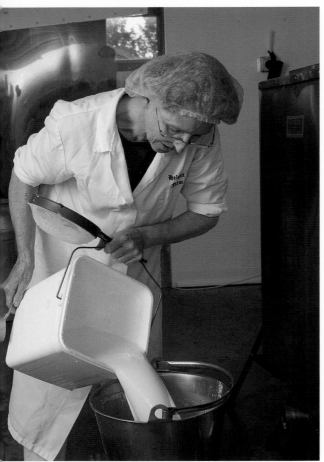

In 2003, not content with producing a range of exotically flavoured, old-fashioned ice creams, handmade in small batches using the best, natural ingredients, Sarah Talbot-Ponsonby and her daughter Elia Allen switched to making organic ice cream. This needed months of new research and working with food technologists, as organic ice cream should not contain emulsifiers, stabilizers or any other artifical additives – the ingredients that help create a smooth texture and the slightly oily feel in the mouth that we, unknowingly, associate with almost all mass-produced ice creams. Helsett Farm organic ice cream contains only whole milk, raw cane sugar, clotted cream, skimmed milk powder and egg yolks; the texture may be slightly denser and grainier, but the taste is sensationally good. Flavours range from vanilla to star anise, and rose, cardamon and almond; uncluttered with artificial additives, they are allowed to speak for themselves.

The world of ice cream is confusing: as well as the growing market for genuine, craft products, there are many other 'Cornish' ice creams, some not even made in the county. The choice extends from frozen yoghurt to the best, artisan Cornish ice cream, with a huge range of products, prices and quality in between. Although as Andrew Treleaven said, 'There are not many of us left, it's like the difference between a craft bakery and mass-produced bakery,' at least there are more ice cream makers with a proper passion for their product than a few years ago.

Tasting the best ice cream for the first time is a revelation. What businesses such as Helsett Farm and Treleaven's have achieved is to show that a top-quality, artisan product, made in small quantities, not only sustains a farm business, which in turn manages and conserves the landscape, but has its own niche in an increasingly competitive market.

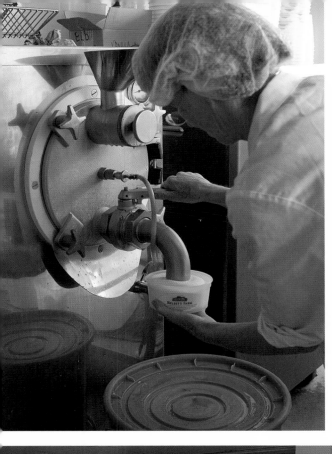

# vanilla ice cream

Although ice cream has been a cheap, mass-produced item since the mid-twentieth century, it has also been reinvented as a quality, craft product sold at the top end of the market. Such has been the rehabilitation of ice cream that in less than ten years it has started to reappear on the menus of top-class hotels and restaurants, no longer just a standby for children, but an integral part of a sophisticated dish. Many chefs now take ice cream so seriously that the very best make their own – a product to be respected and enjoyed in equal measure. It has been restored to the status it had 300 years ago.

This recipe for vanilla ice cream comes from Ben Tunnicliffe of The Abbey in Penzance. One of the youngest chefs in Cornwall to gain a Michelin star, Ben is one of the county's most passionate advocates of using fresh, local and seasonal produce. You could serve this with caramelised rice pudding and rhubarb compote, as at The Abbey, but it is equally good on its own.

## ingredients

*Serves 6*

- 500 ml milk
- 1 vanilla pod
- 10 egg yolks
- 284 g caster sugar
- 1 tsp salt
- 500 ml double

*Above:* Ben Tunnicliffe at The Abbey, Penzance.

## method

Heat the milk in a pan with a tablespoon of the sugar and the salt. Split the vanilla pod lengthways, scrape out the seeds and add with the pod to the milk. Bring gently to the boil, stirring occasionally.

Remove from the heat, cover with clingfilm, and leave to stand for at least 30 minutes for the vanilla to infuse.

Put the milk back on the heat and bring gently back to the boil.

Whisk the remaining sugar and the egg yolks together until pale in colour. When the milk boils, pour half on to the yolks and sugar and mix well. Pour the mixture back into the pan and heat very gently, stirring constantly until cooked. (If you use a thermometer, the temperature will be 65°C, otherwise cook until almost twice the thickness of double cream.) Alternatively, you can do this in either a double boiler or a bowl set over a pan of simmering water, which avoids any chance of the mixture curdling.

Once cooked, add the double cream, sieve and cool. When cool, churn in an ice cream machine, or pour into a suitable container and place in the freezer, removing every 20 minutes to beat until it has set.

# 8 real bread revival

Bread is the universal staff of life, but in the Western world in the last 150 years it has become a debased and largely undervalued food. One of the consequences of the industrial revolution is that 80 per cent of the bread we eat in Britain is mass produced by a small number of multinational milling and baking conglomerates. Even if not always wrapped in plastic, some might say that eating the average white sliced loaf is the equivalent of eating plastic, since it is soft, flavourless and pretty pliable.

Many traditional bakeries disappeared in the 1960s and 1970s as the supermarkets swept across the country, squeezing the life blood out of town centres, but in recent years a quiet revolution has taken place. Like the Campaign for Real Ale, renewed interest in real bread and baking has encouraged a new generation of craft bakers to make modern and traditional breads. Responding to the growing interest in speciality food, increasingly cosmopolitan tastes, and an obvious disenchantment with pallid, soggy sliced loaves, these artisan bakers use small-scale production methods to create innovative, real bread.

Cornwall has been luckier than many other parts of England as its geography delayed both the march of the giant retailers through this long, narrow county and the decline of the high-street baker. There are supermarkets of course, but the county probably retains a higher number of family-run, genuine bakeries than any other part of England. There are more than 150 independent bakers' and confectioners' outlets, ranging from Warrens, set up in 1860 and one of the oldest companies still baking in Cornwall, to H. Pearce in Kelly Bray, where Michael Pearce's bread and saffron cakes use recipes unchanged for three generations. Others with long reputations for excellent bread, cakes and Cornish pasties include W.C. Rowe, Malcolm Barnecutt, the Lostwithiel Bakery, and so on. Few other

*Right:* Loaves and rolls made by Toby Tobin-Dugan, at St Martin's Bakery, Isles of Scilly.

English counties could boast more than 25 different names for a standard tin-loaf, depending on location within the county.

While traditional bakers continue to disappear, the number of modern artisan bakers is gradually increasing. Although most are minute in scale, such as Rachel Carter at Promises and Pie Crusts, or Lydia's Cottage Industries, they produce a range of interesting new breads and elevate bread to an art form, a meal in itself for which we are sometimes prepared to pay more than £2 a loaf, compared with 30p for its rapidly baked, factory-made cousin. Although only a small proportion of the bread baked in the county contains genuine Cornish ingredients, the range of bread available is truly astonishing.

*Below:* Rachel Carter's roast vegetable focaccia.
*Bottom:* Blue Mango, Truro.
*Right:* Toby Tobin-Dugan with a *pain de campagne.*

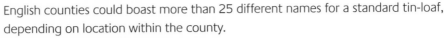

One of the most exciting of the new breed of bakers is Linda Tonkin at Blue Mango, based in the redeveloped Lemon Street Market in Truro. Her bread is not cheap, but it is a fantastic eating experience – real artisan baking. Linda, a former chef, decided to return to Cornwall to bring up her young family. It was only after finding that she could not buy the sort of bread she wanted that she decided to bake speciality bread. Blue Mango produces more than 30 different types of bread: on any one day the selection could include five seeded boules, 100 per cent stoneground with mixed seeds, 100 per cent German rye and caraway, plain white (good for toast as the label claims), French fougasse with hazelnut and sultanas, muffins (lemon and crème fraiche or rhubarb and custard), Moroccan chickpea flat bread heavy with cumin and coriander, and fresh socca – a savoury pancake made with chick pea flour, extra virgin olive oil and water. Linda's principles are proudly proclaimed in this tiny shop: ingredients are sourced with provenance and quality in mind, using local and organic produce if possible. The doughs are left to prove and rise naturally in their own time, often overnight. No flour enhancers or preservatives are used. The result is a feast for the eyes, a shop full of delicious aromas, and tastes which make it impossible to leave without a heavy basket and a lighter purse.

Toby Tobin-Dugan, on St Martin's in the Isles of Scilly, is another craft baker with a single-minded passion for the mystique that surrounds the interaction between yeast, air, flour and

water that creates bread. Like Blue Mango, the St Martin's Bakery is a young business, set up from scratch in 1999. It may be small-scale, but its reputation is such that there is no shortage of customers. It too follows artisan principles, where the weighing, scaling and moulding are done carefully by hand. Sourdough bread, for instance, is left to develop for 24 hours, and Toby keeps back a small amount of leaven to use for the next day's baking – a technique perfected hundreds of years ago. On a busy day at the height of the season he can bake up to 60 loaves, as well as 200 rolls, croissants, *pains aux raisins*, quiches, tarts, cookies and Cornish pasties. Despite the island location, Toby Tobin-Dugan uses as many local ingredients as possible – a combination of his own fruit, herbs and vegetables, tomatoes and cucumber from St Mary's, Tresco beef for his pasties, and fish straight from the sparkling clear seas on his doorstep. The vital missing ingredient is flour milled from Cornish wheat.

*Below:* Linda Tonkin's hazlenut fougasse.
*Top right:* Sign for St Martin's Bakery, Isles of Scilly.
*Bottom right:* Toby Tobin-Dugan's *pain de campagne.*
*Pages 116–17:* Oat stooks, West Penwith.

Corn of various types has been grown in Cornwall since the Celts built ancient field systems more than 3,000 years ago, traces of which can still be found in parts of West Cornwall. It is pretty certain that in these fields the early farmers would have grown primitive forms of oats, rye, *pillas* (similar to rye but with a finer straw, it was used for a kind of porridge, called 'gurts') and wheat. Wheat and rye would have been coarsely ground, usually between two large stones or querns, and made into a rudimentary bread. It would have been solid, flat, unleavened, and baked on a stone in the centre of the fire until hard. While not particularly palatable to modern tastes, this would have been a major part of the early settlers' diet. As they became more sophisticated, breads were made from oat, wheat, rye or barley flours. Naturally leavened, sourdough bread was developed well before yeasted breads became commonplace. By the fifteenth century ale-barm, or sometimes beer itself, were also used to leaven bread.

By the time of the Norman Conquest, milling techniques had developed considerably – the earliest water mill had been built at least 300 years earlier and the Domesday Book records 5,624 water-powered mills in England – so flour would have been stone-ground between two mill stones. The mill at Cotehele is the only surviving working water mill in Cornwall. After a gap of 38 years it was restored to full working order in 2002 and grinds wheat for flour that is used

in the National Trust's restaurant at the Tudor house. However, local water flow difficulties restrict milling to two days a week.

As milling techniques improved so did the flour, which started to be sifted and refined to give a whiter flour. This led to a changing social status for bread: *manchet*, made from finer, expensive wheat flour, from which most of the bran was removed, was so sought after by the rich that special bakeries were set up specializing in fine bread. In London in 1304 there were 32 bakers making brown bread and 21 baking white; by 1574 there were 36 brown-bread bakers and 62 making only white bread.

The majority of the population, particularly in Cornwall, continued eating *maslin* – a dark bread that was coarser, cheaper and less appetizing – or barley bread. *Maslin* was usually made with a mixture of wheat and rye flours, and occasionally bean or pea flour would be added. Cornish kettle bread was a type of sourdough bread made from barley meal, using a leaven kept from the previous week's baking. The 'kettle' referred to the iron pot covering it during baking.

According to Richard Carew there was a shortage of bread and corn in the fifteenth and sixteenth centuries, and without the decline of tin mining, Cornish cereal growing would not have developed as it did:

But when the tin works began to fail and the people to increase, this double necessity drove them to play the good husbands and to provide corn of their own. Labour brought plenty, plenty cheapness, and cheapness sought a vent [sale] beyond the seas ...

Although wheat had previously been grown, it was limited to areas of good land such as the North Cornwall coastal area between Stratton and Padstow, described by John Leland in 1542 as 'very fertile of grass and corn'. As Carew noted, merchants knew that exporting was more profitable than selling at home, until trade was brought to a halt by the Spanish Armada. So it was only barley bread that came between many Cornish families and starvation. Barley was easier to grow and was half the price of wheat. Rye would also grow on poorer ground, but even these cereals could fail in the worst harvests.

*Above:* H. Pearce, Kelly Bray.

Preparing land for cultivation was hard work as much of it was poor and badly needed improvement. Large quantities of sea-sand and seaweed were used, particularly in coastal areas and on the poorer uplands, where the soil was so infertile that after two wheat crops and two of oats it had to be left to lie fallow for seven or eight years.

Early baking techniques soon evolved into a covered system using inverted pots to cover the dough. Piling up ashes around the pot helped draw the bread upwards, giving slightly risen, lighter loaves, although still unleavened. During the fifteenth and sixteenth centuries some homes started to have rudimentary ovens of their own – usually a cloam oven. This and the flat-iron (known as baking under) method were used in Cornish kitchens for hundreds of years.

Cloam (or clome) ovens were made of clay, and were either built into the side of a hearth or free-standing. They were heated by burning bundles of fuel, usually gorse, blackthorn or wood. When the oven was hot the ashes would be removed and the bread put inside, the small front opening covered up, and the bread left to bake in the oven's residual heat. This may explain why today gorse grows so abundantly across the county, now that it is no longer used as fuel.

The flat iron was a large flat piece of iron placed on a three-legged trivet (a brandis). A fire would be lit underneath and when the iron was hot the fire would die down and the iron would be dropped into the ashes (by removing the brandis). The food to be baked, usually bread or pasties, would be put on the hot iron, covered by a large, domed iron baker or 'kettle' (looking like a large frying pan without a handle), and the hot ashes piled up around this.

Families who had only an open hearth were obliged to pay for their bread to be baked either in the manor house's oven, or by the village bakery. Baking methods remained unchanged in some rural areas until the 1930s, when it was still quite common to cook over open peat fires. Many people continued to rely on the local bakehouse to cook their pasties and cakes because 'you couldn't get the slab hot enough' as one elderly cook recalled. A tray of Cornish pasties would cost a penny ha'penny (just over 1/2p) to bake.

The history of Cornish food is full of references to bread riots and food short-ages. One of the earliest recorded total harvest failures, due to bad weather, was in 1315–16. In 1789, as the French Revolution began, there were bread riots in Truro. In the following years, war with France was good for farmers as demand for meat and grain in Plymouth increased, but it was bad for Cornish working men and their families because it forced up prices. War exacerbated existing imbal-ances between supply and demand and drove up food prices in general, as much was commandeered for the Army and Navy, leaving unscrupulous merchants and millers to manage the market to their advantage.

According to A.K. Hamilton Jenkin:

during the worst times of scarcity the poor in the maritime districts
are said to have subsisted almost wholly on limpets and other coarse
shell-fish gathered from the rocks, whilst snails were even used to make
the 'broth' which has ever been a stand-by in the Cornishman's diet.

No wonder there were almost constant riots in a population that was literally starving.

There were frequent riots from 1789 onwards, including 1793, 1794–5, and 1801 – when the *Cornwall Gazette* reported that there were disturbances in every town and village from the Tamar to Land's End. During the 1840s the shortages of bread and corn coincided with the Irish potato famine, and the worst rioting took place during the hard winter of 1846–7, even though the Corn Laws had been repealed in 1846. Introduced in 1815, this legislation had prohibited any imports of foreign corn, protecting farmers by artificially inflating the price of home-grown corn, but also creating shortages which, when harvests failed, ended in riots and anarchy.

The overall improvement in Cornish farming from the late eighteenth and early nineteenth centuries benefited men and crops. Seaweed and sea-sand, already used as soil improvers, and waste from fish processing, or fish that was damaged and unfit for sale, were good sources of fertilizer. By 1811, G.B. Worgan estimated that one-third of the cultivated land was used for wheat, oats, barley and turnips, and as the century progressed the growing numbers working in the booming tin and copper mines, and the effects of the industrial revolution, encouraged farmers to increase grain production. Much of the new land under cultivation was farmed by miners themselves, as well as by enterprising yeoman farmers and land-owners. The Bude Canal, completed in 1825, was used for transporting sea-sand inland, and in 1834 the Bodmin and Wadebridge railway opened to carry sea-sand to farming districts for soil improvement.

However, the industrial revolution brought other changes that had a profound effect on milling and baking, which changed beyond recognition into highly mechanized processes. Huge roller mills working at high speeds could handle large quantities of grain to produce finer, whiter flour, which required different, industrialized baking techniques, which eventually, in the 1930s, spawned the Wonderloaf, the first pre-sliced white, wrapped loaf.

The new, faster baking processes needed flour with higher gluten levels, so soft home-grown wheat was replaced by imported, North American hard wheat. This, and the exodus of miners and their families as mining declined at the end of the nineteenth century, forced many Cornish farmers to switch from cereal growing to dairy farming, which remains one of the county's dominant agricultural sectors.

The industrial revolution also encouraged more independent bakers to expand, and to manufacture bread, cakes and confectionery on a larger scale, By the end of the nineteenth century many bakers, like dairies, had daily delivery rounds. Bread rounds, first by pony and trap, later by van, lasted until the 1950s or early 1960s.

The later development of rapid steam baking, and the so-called Chorleywood process, have created a market dominated by cheap, white (mostly) factory-made bread, where, for a time, even brown bread was made from white flour with added colourings rather than genuine wholewheat flour.

In 1976, the legendary food writer Elizabeth David summed up the irony of the modern British bread industry:

For centuries the working man envied the white bread of the privileged. Now he may very soon grow to envy them their brown wholewheat bread. This is certainly every bit as inaccessible to the majority as was the fine white manchet bread of the sixteenth century... [as] there are very few bakers who make or sell the genuine article.

She would have been thrilled to see the slow recovery of craft baking in Britain.

Despite wheat, rye and barley having been grown successfully for bread-making for hundreds of years, and with the exception of a brief period during the 1930s and the Second World War, when the bakers were forced to use home-grown wheat for flour, little British wheat is used for mass-produced bread. The multinational companies that dominate milling and baking have created a culture in which few British farmers are encouraged to grow milling wheats for bread.

The Trescowthick Craft Bakery, however, is trying to buck this trend by showing that bread can be made using Cornish grain. The family farm and bakery has successfully grown milling wheat on the north Cornish coast near Newquay since 2003. In 2004 a mill was installed to grind this wheat for use in bread, cakes and biscuits, all baked on the premises. Other products from the farm, including meat, eggs and vegetables are used in a range of baked products and ready meals. The entire Buscombe family helps with growing, baking, packaging or sales – on a Saturday selling between 500 and 600 loaves at Truro Farmers' Market.

The baker's life, like those of fishermen and farmers, is not an easy one: the hours are long and the work is hard. But without men and women like Michael Pearce, Linda Tonkin and Toby Tubin-Dugan, who are passionate about their craft, we would not have access to such high-class, top-quality breads and baked goods. Only a dedicated few are prepared to get up and start baking in the early hours of the morning, to make sure that fresh bread is waiting for the rest of us when we start our 'normal' working day.

*Below:* The Trescowthick Craft Bakery at Truro Farmers' Market.

# irish soda bread

This recipe for Irish Soda bread comes from Toby Tobin-Dugan at St Martin's Bakery. Having an Irish grandfather, it seemed appropriate for Toby to develop this recipe to sell in the bakery on Moo Green. Soda bread does not use yeast, and it is quick and easy to bake. The rise is achieved by the effects of combining the cream of tartar, bicarbonate of soda and sour milk or buttermilk. Baking the bread using a metal or ceramic cover revisits the traditional method used for Cornish kettle bread, which was baked in a similar way.

## ingredients

*Makes one loaf*

- 450 g flour (Toby usually uses a 50:50 mix of wholemeal and soft white)
- 1/4 tsp salt
- 1/4tsp sugar
- 1/4 tsp bicarbonate of soda
- 1/4 tsp baking powder
- 1/4 tsp cream of tartar
- 1 egg
- 300 ml buttermilk, or sour milk and water

*Above:* St Martin's Bakery, Isles of Scilly.

## method

Heat oven to 200°C (gas 6).

Mix together flours, salt and sugar in a bowl. Mix together the bicarbonate of soda, baking powder and cream of tartar and add to the flour, combining thoroughly to spread the bicarbonate of soda, baking powder and cream of tartar evenly through the flour.

Without wasting any time – the raising agents will be reacting already – whisk the egg, keeping a little of it aside for glazing, with the buttermilk or soured milk mix, and add briskly to the flour to create a sticky dough.

Shape into a round and glaze with the remainder of the egg. Roughly scatter a liberal handful of flour over the loaf, and slash a cross almost through it. This allows the loaf to cook right through and gives that distinctive Irish soda bread quadrant look.

Bake in a moderate oven for 30 minutes on a greased tray, covered with an ovenproof bowl or metal pot to distribute the heat evenly. Remove the pot or bowl and cook for a further ten minutes to finish off the loaf and give a rich brown colour inside the scored cross.

*Author's note:* I usually use a loose-bottomed cake tin, without the bottom, to cover the dough. If you don't have buttermilk or sour milk, a mixture of milk and water can be substituted. You could include a spoonful of yoghurt to add acidity.

# 9 a cornish icon

When Adam Woolfitt and I were discussing the title for this book, someone suggested 'More than just pasties...'. But the Cornish pasty is a subject dear to the hearts of thousands of resident and expat Cornish men and women, and this title might have been misunderstood. So I thought better of it, but as I hope this book will show, contemporary Cornish foods that are exciting, modern and based on the best Cornish ingredients can co-exist harmoniously alongside traditional foods that have been the backbone of Cornish cuisine for hundreds of years.

So we come to the Cornish pasty. If you are what you eat, or if a food reflects the culture of a country, then the pasty is clearly a Cornish icon, the quintessential Cornish food, known the world over. So much has been said and written about the pasty that it is not easy to find anything new or innovative, except perhaps that the mining and farming families under whose care it evolved into today's familiar shape and form, might be surprised to find that their staple diet has become a widely available, fashionable, fast food that is enjoying a new image and lease of life in an era of grazing, eating on the move, and ready meals.

For hundreds of years most Cornish families existed on a make-do-and-mend type of diet, so it is not surprising that lists of historic recipes include many pies. The pastry would fill hungry stomachs, eking out any scarce bits of meat or using the few available vegetables to make a more interesting and nourishing dish. Two hundred years ago nothing was too big, too small or too unpalatable to be used in a Cornish pie: taddago and lammy pies, for instance, used unmentionable meats and parts of the carcase; curlew, giblet, conger, ram, tatty, lickey (leek) and herby pies all appeared regularly.

So it was almost inevitable that the Cornish pasty should become the equivalent of a national dish. It is treated with a deep, Cornish pride – served with

*Right:* A Cornish icon known the world over, Cornish pasties are traditionally eaten out of a paper bag.

great reverence by Cornish expats all around the world, as well as in almost every Cornish household, following recipes that have been jealously guarded and passed from generation to generation. Search the Internet and you will find Cornish pasty bakers and manufacturers in Yorkshire, Cumbria and Northamptonshire. Groups with ancient Cornish roots proudly swap pasty tales and recipes in Mexico, South Africa and Australia. The association between the pasty and Cornwall links the two words in a way that, say, 'Scotch' and 'egg' cannot, creating passions, memories and emotions. Most consumers genuinely believe that if it is called a Cornish pasty, a pasty must only come from Cornwall. Few other foods evoke this strength of feeling, ownership or interest.

While researching this book Adam and I ate many pasties from many different sources and, it has to be admitted, many different flavours in addition to the traditional version. We each had our own, different, favourite. In the end the decision about who makes the best is subjective and highly personal. More than three million pasties are manufactured in Cornwall each week – the majority for consumption outside the county – many in large factories, others in small craft bakeries, so variations, even within the same bakery, are inevitable and may simply be due to the baker having an off day.

The visitor to Cornwall cannot avoid noticing that pasties are the fast food of choice, followed by fish and chips. Wander around any Cornish town or village and the chances are that at least one shop, café or bakery sells Cornish pasties. At lunchtime, the best have queues of eager customers buying pasties. In fact many bakers would admit that without Cornish pasties their businesses might not be as busy as they are – given the influence of the supermarkets on the overall structure of the high street and our shopping patterns.

*Below:* Cornish pasties for sale in the West Cornwall Pasty Co. at Paddington station, London. Note the range of flavours.

It is difficult to distinguish what makes a good Cornish pasty. Peer into pasty shops in Cornwall and elsewhere, and you will see a range of different fillings and flavours – some good, some interesting, and some truly terrible. It is all a matter of personal choice. Some traditionalists argue strongly against introducing contemporary ingredients such as ricotta (in spinach and ricotta pasties)

or sun-dried tomatoes. Others believe it is only right that there should be a pasty to suit all tastes. Nevertheless, the traditional Cornish pasty will always take pride of place and remains the best-selling variety.

Although the purists argue that a pasty should only be made using beef, potatoes, swede (or turnip as it is known in the county), onion, salt and pepper, a quick search through old Cornish cookery books reveals that pasties were made from anything that was readily to hand. As with many other contemporary culinary trends, it seems the modern craze for multi-flavoured pasties is nothing new. I have recently seen Balti-flavoured pasties, Stilton and leek, chicken curry, vegetarian, and beef and Stilton, although personally I would draw the line at an English breakfast pasty or a chicken tikka-flavoured pasty – surely too much of a cross-cultural mix there?

*Top:* The West Cornwall Pasty Co., Paddington station, London.
*Above:* The latest fast-food craze? Outside the West Cornwall Pasty Co., Covent Garden, London.

Perhaps what is most important is the number of pasty outlets springing up all over the rest of Britain – in motorway service stations, on railway concourses and in central London, for example – that are supplied or run by Cornish companies who make their pasties in Cornwall, blast freeze them, and sell them up country to be baked-off *in situ*. The Crantock Bakery has taken this even further. The company was the first to export pasties to America, and is supplying a new pasty franchise with two outlets in Berlin, one in the Potsdamer Platz, close to the Brandenburg Gate. Could the Cornish pasty be the next international fast-food craze? Competition for the ubiquitous McDonald's?

Although the pasty's recipe and its evolution are undoubtedly Cornish, other foreign foods share the idea of folding a dough or pastry wrapper around other ingredients – Italian *calzone* or South American *empanadas*, for example. The history of the pasty goes back hundreds of years, and the pasty is mentioned by some of England's greatest writers – Chaucer, Shakespeare and Samuel Pepys. In Middle English the word pasty meant 'made of paste', i.e. pastry. The *Oxford English Dictionary* suggests it appeared in around 1300, when a pasty was described as a raised pie using any type of meat. The words 'pie' and 'pasty' were, at that stage, interchangeable. Falstaff, in Shakespeare's *The Merry Wives of Windsor* (1597), invited his guests to dine on venison pasties, and 70 years later the diarist Samuel Pepys remarked on sharing a venison pasty at dinner with friends:

we dined at the Bull head upon the best venison pasty that ever I eat of in my life; and with one dish more, it was the best dinner I ever was at.

For centuries the pasty was a rich, exotic dish served in Royal palaces and other noble houses. Ingredients would include meat or fish, herbs, spices and other delicacies such as truffles, artichokes, oysters and fruit. The pasty was also used as a vehicle for preserving meat. Baking in a heavy-duty pastry case gave the meat

*Below:* Beef cattle at Kestle Farm, mid-Cornwall.

a longer life and made it more portable. Prosperous families would take a meat pasty as a gift to friends or relations, the size and quality of the contents being an overt way of showing off their wealth and status. At the table the pastry would be broken off and usually discarded. A rare eighteenth-century recipe book, belonging to the Polwhele family and now in the Cornwall Record Office, includes recipes for a venison pasty, and another that used beef rump, soaked in claret, seasoned with salt, pepper and nutmeg, covered with a pound of butter, enclosed in pastry and then baked.

During the late eighteenth and early nineteenth centuries, meat was a luxury for most Cornish families, and until that time pasties had been eaten almost exclusively by the affluent and privileged. Gradually the dish transformed into the familiar Cornish pasty, becoming a staple food of poor working families, based on anything that was available, mostly vegetables, wrapped in a pastry crust and slowly baked on an iron sheet, covered with an iron baker. The *hoggan*, consisting of a lump of unleavened dough containing vegetables and, occasionally, green pork, was probably the forerunner of the modern Cornish pasty.

As mining prospered and families started to earn more money – in the 1830s the average working man's wage was 7s. (35p) a week, but a miner working below ground on the tribute system would have earned considerably more

– meat started to feature more regularly in pasties. It was during this industrial boom that the pasty probably evolved into the now familiar D-shaped, filled pastry case. The crust needed to be strong enough to withstand the journey to work and the descent into the tin and copper mines. One view is that the sealed outer edge, or crimp, effectively became a handle, so that a miner could eat the pasty with his arsenic-covered hands (arsenic was a by-product of tin and copper mining) without poisoning himself.

Although the historic details vary from place to place, there is no doubt that what we know as the Cornish pasty eventually became standardized to comprise beef, onion, potato and swede, seasoned only with salt and pepper. The two key ingredients, beef and potato, were crops easily produced and grown in Cornwall. By the end of the nineteenth century, pasties were mass-produced as a basic food for farm workers, miners and their families (probably fishermen too, but there were and still are many superstitions attached to taking pasties to sea), yet the word Cornish, in association with the pasty, was mostly used by people outside the county.

The exodus of Cornish mining skills from the 1840s onwards led to the world-wide spread of pasties as a food item. For the descendants of those original emigrants to Australia, South Africa, Canada and America the Cornish pasty is deeply embedded in their memories, and they jealously guard its recipe and traditions. There is also a small enclave of pasty *aficionados* in Japan – who learnt their skills from the great Japanese potter Shoji Hamada. Hamada worked for many years with Bernard Leach in St Ives, where he also learnt to make pasties, exporting the recipe and techniques to Japan in 1924.

Each of us has a personal favourite, and a preferred baker. Yet in Cornwall, the traditional recipe still outsells all others by a considerable margin. Even Rick Stein's pâtisserie in Padstow bakes crab and saffron, or cheese and leek pasties in addition to steak pasties. Cornwall has so many excellent pasty-makers that it would be invidious to single out any one particular baker. At one end of the scale are dedicated pasty manufacturers such as Ginsters, Proper Cornish and the West Cornwall Pasty Company; at the opposite

*Below:* Ingredients for a traditional Cornish pasty.
*Right:* Ready for the oven – Ann Muller's pasties at The Lizard Pasty Shop.

end are individual butchers and bakers taking their own approach to one of Corn-wall's most famous and traditional foods.

Try the Gear Farm Shop, or The Lizard Pasty Shop, where Ann Muller has be-come something of a national institution for her pasties – she has also featured in the national press for her stout defence of the Cornish pasty. When the American food writer William Grimes made the mistake of criticizing Cornish pasties in the *New Yorker*, she set fire to an American flag outside her bakery on the Lizard. At the other end of the county Yvonne Rogers, at Sleepy Hollow Farm near Gun-nislake, sells pasties in her farm shop and café, and the lunchtime queues outside Michael Pearce's bakery in Kelly Bray have to be seen to be believed.

Today the Cornish pasty is eaten the world over and is the subject of an application to protect its heritage. While this book was being written, a group of 40 Cornish bakers and pasty manufacturers was applying for a European pro-tected status (the Protected Geographical Indication, or PGI). If they are successful, only pasties made in Cornwall, to the traditional recipe, could be called 'Cornish Pasties'. However, this will not detract from the myriad of other flavoured pasties now available, both in and outside Cornwall. They will still be called pasties, but not *Cornish* pasties. If the PGI designation is granted, the Cornish pasty will be elevated to similar status as Whitstable oysters, Newcastle brown ale and Dorset Blue cheese.

*Left:* Ann Muller's freshly baked pasties.
*Below: A* Cornish pasty – ideal fast food for the surf generation.

Unsurprisingly for a county that annually celebrates hundreds of feasts and festivals, Cornwall has a pasty festival, held at Morvah in August. Pasty Day is also celebrated in the American state of Michigan, where pasties are more popular than hamburgers.

At lunchtime in any Cornish town centre or seaside resort there is a good chance that more than half the people you see will be eating a pasty. Eaten straight from a paper bag (the correct, Cornish method), the pasty takes some beating as the original fast food – a meal in itself.

There are thousands of recipes for pasties, and hundreds of variations on the traditional Cornish pasty recipe. Arguments continue to rage over whether the crimping should be on the side (to form a useful handle), or on the top (to keep the juices in). All recipes agree that the traditional Cornish pasty should contain only beef, potato, onion, swede (often called turnip in Cornwall), salt and pepper. The filling ingredients are always added uncooked. This recipe comes from *Pasties and Cream: Memories and Recipes from a Cornish Childhood*, written by Hettie Merrick. Mrs Merrick is Ann Muller's mother, and she taught her daughter to make pasties. Mrs Merrick maintains that she can recognize Ann's pasties anywhere: 'Every mouthful is a piece of Cornwall – a dream folded in heaven.'

# cornish pasty

## ingredients

*Makes approximately 8 pasties*

Pasty pastry
- 500 g strong white flour (pinch of salt optional)
- 125 g margarine
- 125 g lard
- cold water to mix

Filling for each pasty
- 50 g finely sliced swede (turnip)
- 25 g finely sliced onion
- 175 g sliced potatoes
- 75–100 g Cornish beef (skirt or chuck)
- salt and pepper

*Above:* The Lizard Pasty Shop.

## method

*Pastry:* Put the margarine in the freezer for ten minutes. Place the flour in a bowl and rub in the lard. Grate the margarine and stir into the flour with a knife. Pour in cold water and mix with a knife until absorbed.

Knead the mixture a little and leave it at least half an hour before using, or make it the day before and store in the fridge overnight.

*Filling:* Keep the sliced potatoes in a basin of cold water until needed. Trim off any gristle and cut the meat in 6 mm (1/4 in) pieces, including some fat.

Cut off 100 g of made pastry and shape it roughly like a ball. Roll out into a large round the size of a dinner plate.

Place the onion along the centre of the pastry and cover with a layer of swede. Sprinkle well with pepper and a shake of salt. Place the meat along the top and ends. (The ends are the corners and the cook must make sure that the meat is spread into the corners.) Season the meat with salt. Top this layer with most of the potato, salt lightly and place the remainder of the potato on top.

Moisten the further half of the edge of the pastry with water and fold over to seal. Press the sides of the pasty together, from the middle outwards towards each end, pressing firmly and gently. Crimp the edge from left to right by folding the pastry edge over and over in a rope pattern, tucking in the end when you reach the other side.

Place the pasties apart on a flat baking tray, brush with beaten egg or milk. (Pasties are steam-cooked. Some people make a hole in the top to let the steam out. Mrs Merrick does not.)

Place in a hot oven, 220°C (gas 7), on a shelf three-quarters of the way up, and bake for 15–20 minutes. Check the pasties and if they are brown move to a lower shelf and turn oven down to 180°C (gas 4) and cook for a further 25 minutes. Then turn the oven off altogether and leave the door shut for a further ten minutes. Remove from oven and allow to rest before serving.

# 10 sugar and spices

In the 1840s, while poor tinners and working men were rioting in the streets of Truro and Launceston, or queuing at soup kitchens in St Austell and Redruth, in genteel drawing rooms, ladies were following the new fashion of taking afternoon tea. Yet Cornwall's strong tradition of what we now think of as tea-time treats – most famously cream teas and saffron cake – followed by fairings and hevva (heavy) cake, has a longer history than the dainty sandwiches and small cakes that were served when Anna, Duchess of Bedford, decided that the gap between luncheon and dinner was too long and invited friends to join her for tea and cakes.

Yeast breads developed gradually in the fifteenth and sixteenth centuries, using leftover dough to which spices and dried fruits were added. The leavening agent was barm or ale, modern yeast appearing only in the 1850s. The first recipe for saffron cake and buns appeared in a sixteenth-century recipe book, *The Receipt Book* by Lady Fettiplace, and Sir Kenelm Digby gave a recipe in 1669 for rich yeast bread using butter, milk, sugar, currants, raisins, saffron and other spices. Yeast-based cakes were also a popular banqueting food, while spiced buns filled with caraway seeds, raisins or currants were made specifically for Lent.

By the end of seventeenth century, better-off Cornish families were using the 'bake under' method to cook biscuits, cakes, buns and puddings beneath a 'kettle' – an iron dome similar to a large frying pan. For special occasions great cakes, yeasted and filled with fruit and spices, were made. Soon after that the upper classes were eating spiced breads and cakes, with butter, at breakfast and some-times as a late afternoon or early evening snack with a glass of wine. By the end of the eighteenth century cakes and biscuits were also on their lunchtime menu.

Numerous regional variations of spiced and fruited loaves and cakes developed, many of which remain today – saffron cake, bara brith in Wales and Lincolnshire

*Right:* A tray of saffron buns ready for the oven, made by Michael Pearce of Kelly Bray.

## saffron

The theory of how and when saffron first came to Cornwall is still a subject of hot debate. The most popular – although disputed and supported in almost equal measure by both historians and food writers – is that it arrived with the Phoenicians, who were trading saffron and other goods for Cornish tin from about 1000 BC.

Recent pottery finds in Tintagel suggest there were strong trading links with the Eastern Mediterranean and North Africa between the fifth and seventh centuries, and by AD 960 the Arabs were cultivating saffron in Spain, another important Cornish trading partner, where some of the finest and most sought-after saffron is still grown.

Saffron was grown extensively in Persia, Turkey and Kashmir, so it is quite likely that after the Crusades the warrior knights and pilgrims to the Holy Land smuggled the bulbs, or corms, back to England. Later pilgrims travelling through Spain to the shrine of St James in Santiago de Compostela could have returned with either dried saffron or the bulbs, which legend suggests they hid in their staves.

Whatever its route to Britain, by the Middle Ages this highly valued spice – also used as a dye and for medicinal purposes – was a popular ingredient in grand kitchens. Saffron was highly prized for its aroma, and for colouring and flavouring. It was used in sauces, cordials, possets and stews, and would have been used with other spices to disguise poor quality ingredients,

The world's most expensive spice, in the fourteenth century saffron commanded 14s (70p) per oz (28 g), compared with £59.75 for 10 g in 2004, which no doubt added to its cachet as a highly desirable ingredient. However, only tiny amounts are needed to create the deep yellow colour and distinctive taste: too much results in a taste akin to dry-cleaning fluid.

The saffron crocus (*Crocus sativus*) is extremely labour-intensive to cultivate. Each autumn the flower stamens are carefully harvested by hand as the bulbs flower. The dried filaments of about 70,000 flowers are needed for one pound (450g) of dried saffron.

For almost 300 years Saffron Walden in Essex was the acknowledged centre of British saffron growing, changing its name to reflect the importance of the crop. But records show that there was earlier, small-scale cultivation in fifteenth-century herb gardens. Saffron was also grown in Launcells, near Bude in North Cornwall, and there were so-called saffron meadows at Fowey, Penryn, Feock and Gerrans. However, it is unclear whether it was saffron in these fields or other yellow crops, bearing in mind that *Crocus sativus* has a purple flower, and the Middle English word for yellow was *safron*. In the sixteenth century, saffron was a profitable crop, yielding £40 per acre.

During the last 100 years a combination of cost, wartime rationing and industrialized food manufacturing led many commercial businesses to take short cuts, using yellow colourings, such as annatto, to give saffron cakes their distinctive hue. The real thing is unmistakeable, and some Cornish bakers deliberately leave saffron strands in the dough as a visual guarantee that they have used the genuine article. Substitutes simply will not do, as the best bakers will tell you.

Cornish chefs have recognized the value of saffron's delicate, heady aroma, and subtle flavourings for dishes such as saffron seafood risotto, or sea bass with saffron sauce, complete its culinary renaissance and restore it to its rightful place in modern Cornish cuisine.

Plum bread – but why the fashion for spiced, saffron cake died out apart from in Cornwall is something of a mystery.

Some of Cornwall's best saffron cakes and buns are made by Michael and Margaret Pearce in Kelly Bray. The Pearce family started baking in Callington in 1865, but by the turn of the century Michael Pearce's grandfather had moved to nearby Kelly Bray to set up on his own. A genuine craft baker, Mr Pearce is an increasing rarity, one of a few bakers still using old-fashioned methods, where much of the work is done by hand, and the doughs are given time to prove and rise slowly.

The simple bakery consists of a couple of wooden work areas where the dough is worked and shaped, a large industrial dough mixer – used intermittently – a steam cabinet, where bread and the golden yellow, currant-stuffed saffron buns are left to rise, and large, gas-fired ovens at the back of the bakery. The adjacent workroom, once Michael Pearce's parents' home, is a confectionery room where a range of confectionery or fancies – biscuits and small cakes such as congress tarts, doughnuts, sponges and iced slices – are baked and finished.

The Pearces' most famous products, saffron cake and buns, are made entirely by hand. The rich dough recipe is a closely guarded secret, unchanged for three generations, and includes butter, sugar, flour, yeast and Spanish saffron. Saffron buns are baked most days, and saffron cake two or three times a week. Mr Pearce,

who was once the Cornish wrestling champion, also makes a similar, plainer dough cake, using less fruit and saffron, bread, pasties, pies and cakes, as well as confectionery.

Although the business has responded to changing tastes, Michael Pearce and the Lostwithiel Bakery are two of a diminishing number of bakers still producing splits – or tuffs as they are known in South East Cornwall and parts of Devon – mostly for special orders. Made from sweetened yeast dough, splits are the traditional ingredient of a Cornish cream tea (see also Chapter 5), although most commercial tearooms substitute scones – frowned upon by traditionalists as a Devon habit! A light mouthful of slightly sweet, soft crumb that is somewhere between bread and cake, splits are the perfect vehicle for cream and jam.

The cream tea is, of course, one of the quintessential Cornish treats, and is recognized as a specific West Country speciality. Its main ingredient, clotted cream, has a long history. By the seventeenth century, clotted cream was used for cooking, served with sweet dishes, on bread or other baked goods. The cream tea in its modern form seems to have developed during the nineteenth century, coinciding with better access to cheaper imported sugar (for jams and preserves) and the development of tea as a regular meal. Cornish cream teas were the ideal treat to offer the growing number of tourists visiting the county, who enjoyed them in tea gardens in places such as Marazion, Saltash and Bude. In 1893, Penzance had at least seven refreshment rooms serving teas.

Although the concept of afternoon tea is relatively new, one Cornish tea-time treat, fairings, probably has the oldest history of all, going back to the medieval hiring fairs. Originally a term to describe sweet biscuits and other sweetmeats sold at these fairs, the first

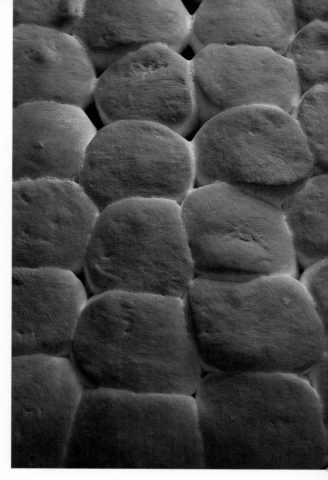

*Left:* Michael Pearce and Roger Canham preparing Cornish splits.
*Above:* Cornish splits.
*Below:* Hevva, or heavy cake (see page 144).

## feast days and festivals

It was Parson Robert Hawker, the vicar of Morwenstow in North Cornwall, who revived the Harvest Festival in 1843, but this was only one in a long tradition of Cornish religious festivals stretching back hundreds of years. The Harvest Festival was quite distinct from harvest suppers, which had been celebrated for over 400 years on individual farms, after all the crops had been successfully gathered in, later becoming village events.

In the sixteenth century, Richard Carew noted that Whitsun was regularly celebrated with church ales (see Chapter 14) and an elaborate communal feast, and that many parishes also marked their own feast day. By the end of the nineteenth century, this was often a two-day annual celebration of the church's patron saint, starting in church on Feast Sunday and ending with a public holiday in the parish on Feast Monday, with much feasting for the whole community. In some villages where parish feasts are still celebrated, children have the day off school.

During the nineteenth and twentieth centuries, chapel and faith teas became regular events where the whole parish would gather and enjoy elaborate teas. Chapel teas would be provided by the parish, while in the case of faith teas each family would bring a plate of food to share. Tea treats were also popular in Cornish towns and villages. Originally religious processions tied to the chapel or Sunday School, led by the local band and accompanied by hymns, the climax was a wonderful tea, with every child given a tea treat bun – a large saffron bun up to 12 inches in diameter. These were important events in Cornish life, given that even after the 1871 Bank Holidays Act, until relatively recently most workers had little paid holiday. Feast days are still celebrated, but the number of parishes enjoying this annual ritual has declined compared with 100 years ago, when one would occur somewhere in Cornwall almost every week of the year. St Just in Penwith, for example, has a week-long festival traditionally timed to coincide with the opening meet of the Western hunt, at the beginning of November. Further north, feast days are known as revels and are celebrated in a similar way, often including a grand tea featuring splits, clotted cream, saffron cake, hevva or yeast cake or buns. Across the county, the number of chapels that have been converted into desirable residences is evidence of the general decline of religion, and both Anglican and Methodist congregations are dwindling fast. But for the time being a few chapel and faith teas survive, particularly in the most remote rural areas where, as one person tactfully said, 'people still cook the old fashioned way'.

Cornwall's most famous festivals are, without doubt, Padstow's Obby Oss Day, on May Day, and Helston's Flora Day, with the Furry Dance as its highlight. Both festivals came close to dying out during the early twentieth century, but have been revived and reinvigorated. The food connection here? Not only were both festivals thought to have originated as pagan fertility rites to celebrate the coming of spring, and to promote good crops for the year, they were and still are an excuse for a good celebration (see Chapter 14). Many Cornish villages continue to hold smaller May Day festivals; the Summercourt Fair still takes place, and on 23 December, Tom Bawcock's Eve, complete with the traditional Stargazy Pie (see page 16), is celebrated in Mousehole. Probably one of the most important events of the Cornish year today is the Royal Cornwall Show, which is held for three days near Wadebridge in June.

*Right:* The Furry Dance at Helston's Flora Day.

fairings were a derivative of gingerbread, flavoured with honey, saffron, liquorice or sandalwood, decorated with almonds, gold leaf, marzipan or icing. Ginger was a highly prized spice in medieval times and widely used. Bakers' gingerbread would have been available at fairs, and became a popular treat for feast days, enjoyed by rich and poor alike.

By the start of the twentieth century the word 'fairings' was also applied to sugared almonds, macaroons and gingerbreads. It was almost obligatory for young men to buy bags or boxes of fairings to take home to their girlfriends and families. Furniss, set up in Truro in 1886 and now in Pool, grew out of a small family baking business to become the first manufacturer to bake fairings and sugar confectionery on a commercial scale. The company's modern range of biscuits includes Cornish fairings, a slightly spiced biscuit, baked to a secret recipe.

Another Cornish speciality, hevva cake, was not reserved for high days and holidays. Its heritage is probably as old as saffron cake, but it has a simpler recipe. It may well have started as a fuggan – a lump of pastry filled with currants rather than a piece of green pork (in which case it would have been a hoggan, the early antecedent of the Cornish pasty). It then developed into a rolled-out pastry dough containing dried fruit and, on special occasions, was made with clotted cream. The top was marked with a criss-cross pattern, said to represent fishing nets. (Incidentally, old Cornish recipes refer to figs or figgys, which were raisins or currants. Hence figgy hobbin, which is similar to hevva, or heavy cake.)

Whether the name developed as a result of the pilchard huer's cry 'hevva hevva' is open to debate, but the historical explanation of the link to pilchard seining is that hevva cakes were baked as a celebration cake after the women had been paid for their part in bulking up, or layering and salting, the catch. Hevva cake would also have been eaten by farm workers and miners as part of their croust, and later became an essential part of a Cornish high tea.

Given that for hundreds of years the Cornish working man's diet was extremely meagre, consisting mainly of bread, vegetables and some fish, but little meat or dairy produce, it is not surprising that a taste developed for these wonderful spiced breads, cakes, biscuits and sweet dishes that formed the centre piece at parish feasts, birthdays, Christmas and harvest home celebrations and, later, chapel and faith teas, once regularly held in every Cornish village.

A.K. Hamilton Jenkin evokes the hive of activity in a well-off farming family as they prepared for an early nineteenth-century parish feast:

> In addition to the baking of bread, great batches of saffron cake, 'seedy' cake, potato cake, pasties, 'fuggans', and gingerbreads had also to be prepared. In some cases a single buttermilk cake, as large as

*Right:* An old Cornish treat: fairings and a glass of milk.

a coster's cartwheel, and requiring two women to carry it, would be cooked to itself beneath one huge 'baker'. In the midst of all this activity, might be seen the farmer's wife ... with her arms bare to the elbow, she kneaded the huge batches of dough; whilst one of the maids ran back and forth to the dairy and 'spence' (larder), bringing in the 'raw' (fresh) milk, the butter and cream, the eggs, the currants, the nutmeg and the 'sponge' or home-made yeast.

He noted that some parishes had a reputation for the paucity of their feast tables, but added diplomatically that 'every household at that time kept up the feast to the utmost limit of its means.'

Spiced breads and cakes used expensive ingredients and had wonderful textures and flavours that contrasted with the drab monotony of daily meals. Centuries of Cornish sea-trading had introduced dried fruit, and other exotic goods, but often at a price. Smuggling would have made tea, spices and brandy readily available in a county that, even at the start of the nineteenth century, was still remote and isolated from the rest of the country. Sugar was an expensive ingredient: in 1841 it cost 8d. (3p) per lb, compared with a mine-worker's wage of £2 5s. (£2.25) per month, so the poorest families often used treacle (a by-product of sugar refining) instead. This was probably how thunder and lightening – bread or splits with clotted cream and treacle – evolved.

The style of baking and teas was to change, spurred on in the 1850s by the development of modern yeast, self-raising flour and baking powder, followed by the opening of teashops. The Aerated Bread Company (ABC) and Lyons Corner Houses were well established in London by the end of the Victorian era. During Edwardian times tea became part of everyday life for all classes, and in many middle- and working-class homes in Cornwall it became high tea, and was frequently the main or final meal of the day. Unlike the dainty teas served in genteel drawing rooms, tearooms and smart London hotels, this light meal would include cold meat pies, pasties, splits with jam and cream, saffron cake or heavy cake.

In 1929 Edith Martin compiled the first printed Cornish recipe book, *Cornish Recipes Ancient & Modern*, which collected recipes from Women's Institute members all around the county. These reflect the simple workaday diet that most Cornish families had followed for hundreds of years – there are few fancy or sophisticated dishes, no references to madeleines, cream puffs or thinly cut cucumber sandwiches. But there are ten recipes for saffron cake, recipes for seed cake and fuggan, four versions of hevva or heavy cake, and several fruit cake variations, such as Penzance cake or porter cake. Cornish splits (three versions) are here proposed as the authentic vehicle for the cream tea.

Yet by the middle of the twentieth century, traditional cakes were in decline. Much of this was a direct result of the tearoom fashions that favoured iced fancies and scones, and the steady increase of supermarkets and convenience foods. Tearooms like the Lyons Corner Houses sold sponge cakes to take home, which discouraged home baking. A.K. Hamilton Jenkin observed that the Cornish no longer appeared 'to hold their saffron cake in the same regard as formerly, and at the chapel gatherings and Sunday school "treats" its place is surely, if slowly, being taken by the cheaper varieties of "fancy" cakes now sold in the multiple shops.'

Since the mid-1990s there has been something of a revival, encouraged perhaps by the rise of Cornish nationalism and a determination to revive Cornish culture. Almost every commercial

*Top:* Danish pastries, made by Toby Tobin-Dugan, St Martin's, Isles of Scilly. Above: Michael Pearce's fancies.

baker in Cornwall makes saffron cakes and buns, yeast and heavy cake, and the largest are supplying these, and pre-packed Cornish cream teas, to some of the major supermarkets. For many Cornish bakeries, pasties and traditional tea treats have become the main source of revenue. But in most cases mass production does not do these products many favours. Try WI country markets and farmers' markets to sample the genuine, homemade product.

With the revival of interest in Cornish dishes, and while parish feasts, celebrations and chapel teas continue, traditional Cornish tea-time treats, the cream tea in particular, should survive a little longer. But with the rise of the cosmopolitan café culture, the decline of churchgoing and the gradual disintegration of rural life, they face strong competition.

# saffron bread and butter pudding

This recipe comes from Richard James at the Nare Hotel on the Roseland, where it is served as one of a changing menu of hot puddings. It is also a good way of using up leftover saffron cake and butter. The Nare Hotel is passionate about using the best local ingredients wherever possible, so butter comes from nearby Barwick Farm, and clotted cream from Rodda's. The saffron cake is made in the hotel.

## ingredients

### Serves 6–8

- 12 slices saffron cake
- 50 g soft butter
- 8 egg yolks
- 175 g caster sugar
- 1 vanilla pod
- 300 ml milk
- 300 ml double cream
- 25 g sultanas
- 25 g raisins

*Above:* The Nare Hotel.

## method

Grease a 3-pint pudding tray with butter.

Remove the crust from the slices of saffron cake.

Whisk together the egg yolks and caster sugar.

Bring the milk, cream and split vanilla pod up to simmering point, stir well, and then pour on to the egg-yolk mixture, stir and sieve.

Arrange the slices of saffron cake in layers in the prepared tray, sprinkling the sultanas and raisins between the layers, and finishing with a final layer of saffron cake.

Pour the egg custard mix over the layers of saffron cake and fruit, and leave to soak into the mixture for 20 minutes before cooking.

Cook in a bain-marie containing hot water for approximately 30 minutes at 180°C (gas mark 4).

When ready, sprinkle with caster sugar and glaze under a grill.

Serve with Cornish clotted cream.

# 11 catching early markets

One of the joys of driving around the Tamar Valley in early autumn is the number of roadside stalls that still sell fruit and vegetables, picked earlier that day by the valley's few remaining growers. Fresh dewy lettuces sit next to multi-coloured squashes, punnets of late raspberries or strawberries, and bunches of herbs. Specialist greengrocers, like D.L. Tregenza in Penzance, and farm shops dotted around the county have the same abundance of just-harvested produce. A trip one September afternoon to Phil Langdon's Chyreen fruit farm at Carnon Downs yielded runner beans, corn on the cob, parsley, plump yellow courgettes, calabrese, raspberries and strawberries.

The unique mild maritime climate makes the county well suited to growing vegetables. For more than 100 years the combination of good soils and the benefits of the Gulf Stream – severe frosts are rare, and in West Cornwall infrequent snowfall usually disappears in a few hours – gave the county a competitive edge over growers elsewhere, and earlier access to markets for the first potatoes, strawberries and cauliflowers. Horticulture was big in Cornwall. Today much of that advantage has been lost, as cheap aviation fuel has blasted away the climatic gains to provide consumers with year-round access to strawberries, mange-tout peas, and the ubiquitous 'new' potato that is nothing of the sort.

For hundreds of years working families and farm workers either grew or had access to a limited range of green and root vegetables, mostly peas, beans, onions, leeks and, later, potatoes. As horticulture advanced in the 1600s and 1700s,

*Right:* D.L. Tregenza, Penzance.

*Below:* Terracotta forcing pots, Heligan.
*Bottom:* The kitchen garden, Tresillian.

wealthy Cornish landowners started developing kitchen gardens and potagers to provide a year-round abundance of fresh fruit and vegetables. There were large resident families to feed, as well as significant numbers of servants and outside workers, so kitchen gardens were essential for daily supplies of fruit and vegetables. Any surplus was sold at local markets.

The owners of houses like Heligan and Tresillian had the time, enthusiasm and cash to invest in growing as wide a range of exotic produce as possible. Heligan, for example, had pineapple pits, a melon yard and glasshouses for peaches, oranges, bananas and grapes. The nineteenth century was a time of great horticultural development, led by the gardeners of the great country houses. This hive of activity was brought to an end by the First World War, as the gardens at Heligan eloquently testify. At Tresillian (built in 1792), John Harris runs a superbly restored, model walled kitchen garden, growing Victorian varieties of organic fruit and vegetables using his own moon-gardening techniques. Both houses give a unique and detailed insight into Cornish fruit and vegetable production in Victorian times.

The part of the county that still benefits from its position and specific weather conditions is West Cornwall, home of what has become known colloquially as the Cornish Early. This is not a specific potato variety but a generic marketing brand developed in 2003 to promote the earliest new potatoes harvested and sold in Cornwall.

Although the first potatoes probably came to Britain in the 1590s, from South America via Spain, almost 200 years passed before they were generally cultivated and accepted as a vegetable. At first they were treated with suspicion, and used only as an animal feed and substitute for flour when grain was scarce, but by 1775 potatoes were part of the Cornish diet, eaten by rich and poor alike. From then on this valuable food source was grown everywhere, even in raised lazy beds on the moors and in orchards. By 1811, when G.B. Worgan published his survey of Cornish agriculture, potatoes, along with barley, oats, cattle, sheep and pigs were exported out of the county as it grew 'much more than it consumes'.

The early potato rapidly earned a reputation as a seasonal delicacy. In 1808 shipments were going to Bristol, London, Portsmouth and Plymouth. Farmers in West Cornwall and the Isles of Scilly were experimenting with earlier plantings to take advantage of the mild climate, although some historians believe that early potatoes had been a profitable crop for the Scillonians since the seventeenth century. But once the Isles of Scilly flower industry took off in the 1880s, potatoes were relegated to second place, although some businesses struggled on until the last commercial grower gave up in 1999. The parish of Paul, between Newlyn and Mousehole, was once famous for producing two potato crops in one year, due to its sheltered position and 'vicinity to seaweed and sand, concurring with the favourable soil'.

*Above:* Cornish Earlies from West Cornwall. *Pages 154–5:* Cornish Earlies growing under protective plastic on the 'golden mile' near Penzance.

The Cornish Early, like so many other crops in Cornwall, has almost lost its climatic advantage, and has to compete with 'new' potatoes from Israel, Cyprus and Egypt. These are not new at all, but have cornered the market thanks to cheap transport and the invention of the polytunnel. Most of these so-called new potatoes are in fact either small main-crop potatoes or new potatoes grown the previous year, or in polytunnels and put into store. I was once offered 'new' potatoes in a West Cornwall restaurant in January. The owner tried to persuade me that they were not only new but Cornish! They were nothing of the sort, but this illustrates the confusion that has been allowed to creep into food descriptions. If you are offered a new potato between August and April (Cornish or otherwise), reject it, as it will bear no relation to the unique Cornish Early which should be small, almost translucent, soft-skinned, and with a distinctive sweet taste.

Genuine Cornish Earlies are only available for the first few weeks of the new potato season, and growers are using the latest techniques to retain their market advantage. Planting is usually in December or early January, using protective plastic or horticultural fleece to cover the soil to ensure that the first potatoes are ready to lift at the end of April. Catching this brief, early market is still vital to 20 or so farmers in West Cornwall. One or two grow large acreages under contract for supermarkets, others grow anything between five and 40 acres to sell locally.

One advantage of growing early potatoes is that they can be double-cropped with West Cornwall's other best-known vegetable – broccoli. Broccoli in this case is not calabrese but the winter cauliflower, introduced from Europe during Elizabethan times, and usually harvested from September to March. For almost 200 years it has been as important to this part of Cornwall as potatoes, thanks to an ingenious steward on the *Herald*, a passenger ship sailing between Hayle and Bristol. Sharrock Dupen noticed the higher prices cauliflowers were selling for in Bristol's markets, and in 1837 took the first profitable consignment from Hayle to Bristol, setting off the development of what soon became a vital farming activity in West Cornwall. Strawberries, already commercially cultivated, early potatoes and mackerel, according to season, were also sent up the Bristol Channel. By 1859, the *West Briton* reported:

> It may now be safely asserted that not less than from thirty to forty
> thousand dozen of broccoli are sent away in the height of the season
> to different places from the parishes surrounding Penzance.

However, it was the completion of Brunel's Royal Albert Bridge over the Tamar in 1859, and the final change from narrow- to broad-gauge railway, which meant that trains could run straight from Penzance to Plymouth, encouraging a massive expansion of horticulture in West Cornwall, the Isles of Scilly and the Tamar Valley.

Broccoli (cauliflower) harvest.
*Left and top:* At Trenow, the Wallis' family farm, Gulval, near Penzance.
*Above:* First-prize winners at the West Cornwall Spring Show.

Today most of the steep fields along the River Tamar, which forms the border between Devon and Cornwall, have reverted to scrub or woodland compared with the frenetic activity 100 years ago when it was, quite literally, Cornwall's market garden. The valley's proximity to Plymouth, the river boats and good rail links to the rest of the country, made it ideal for growing fruit, flowers and a few vegetables. While not as advanced as the Isles of Scilly or West Cornwall, the area nevertheless benefits from a mild, almost frost-free climate. The sheltered valley is drier and not prone to damaging, salt-laden winds. It also had access to a plentiful supply of labour. Boat building and mining were in decline, so fruit picking or other fieldwork during spring, summer and autumn evenings, were a useful source of extra income.

In 1862 James Lawry visited London and realized that strawberries on sale there were not only more expensive but also several weeks later than in the valley. He returned to Cornwall, and a year later his first strawberry consignment to Covent Garden sold for 2s. 6d per pound – five times the price he could expect at home. Although there was already some growing for local markets, this was the start of the so-called strawberry rush. Encouraged by Lawry, commercial-scale strawberry growing, and later apple and plum orchards (see Chapter 12) took off, as hundreds of growers throughout the valley cleared and cultivated every available piece of the wooded, south-facing land to plant fruit.

As branch-line rail links developed, Tamar Valley strawberries were also sent to Manchester, Edinburgh, the Midlands and local markets including Saltash, where they would be served in the popular tea gardens. Gooseberries, raspberries and rhubarb were also grown, much being sent to Plymouth and Bristol later in the season for jam making. During the Second World War the emphasis switched to growing essential crops such as potatoes and other vegetables.

At its most productive, six parishes in the Tamar Valley, covering 1,000 acres in an area of approximately 13 square miles, produced top fruit, soft fruit, early spring flowers and some vegetables. Many of the intensively cultivated gardens, as they were known, were tiny – a handful of acres would provide a decent living as orchards would be under-planted with flowers, potatoes or other fruit. For almost a century everyone living in the valley had the chance to cash in on the economic bonanza of being the first strawberry producers in the country. Early strawberries and small quantities of other produce could be sent by rail with the confidence that it would arrive safely at the other end – a far cry from twenty-first century volume production, which is highly automated and computerized, and where deliveries to supermarkets are so critically timed that if a driver misses his slot his load may be rejected.

The post-war years have had a major impact on this lovely landscape. Food production became more industrialized and the supermarkets more influential, making the scale of operations in areas like the Tamar Valley inefficient and expensive. The combination of the so-called Beeching cuts – which closed a significant tranche of Britain's railways in the mid-1960s – and cheap air freight rapidly ended the agricultural prosperity of this steep-sided valley. The next generation of growers saw little future in continuing the hard graft on difficult, often near vertical slopes, and drifted

*Below and right:*
Harvesting beetroot and courgettes at Gear Farm on the Lizard.
*Page 160: Top:* Runner beans at Gear Farm.
*Middle:* The Gear Farm Shop.
*Bottom:* Harvesting asparagus at St Erme.

away to better paid jobs in nearby Plymouth, including the Navy, or moved out of the region.

In less than 40 years, the valley's south-facing slopes have become overgrown and eerily silent, no longer echoing with the songs and chatter of men, women and children as they picked daffodils, cherries, strawberries or apples. A small pocket of traditional growing remains, mostly in private hands, on land that is easier to manage, producing a few cherries, strawberries, raspberries, beans, cabbage, rhubarb, lettuce and tomatoes, mostly for local buyers. Specialized growers and nurseries concentrate on plants and foliage – alstroemerias, pinks, anemones, daffodils and narcissi. These bigger commercial businesses rely on glasshouses and polytunnels – a landscape feature that has been present in the Tamar Valley for 100 years, and more recently up and down the county, but whose economic value should be weighed against its visual impact on the countryside.

The development of foreign holidays has affected our culinary tastes and led to a more imaginative and varied diet – not for nothing are our high streets peppered with pizza takeaways and Indian restaurants. The same social factors also shaped Cornwall's tourism industry for a couple of decades. Yet the irony is that as tourism has revived, so has an interest in locally grown and sourced foods – discerning visitors and residents are demanding the very thing that their parents and grandparents eschewed as being unfashionable and uninteresting. We have turned a full circle, yet the shackles of modern conveniences make it difficult to return to or reinvent precisely those things that we now recognize as having some value.

However, a growing number of producers are responding to this new impetus, reviving the market-gardening principle to supply local markets. Dave Webb on the Lizard is one example, growing a large range of organic vegetables, herbs and salad crops, mostly to sell in the Gear Farm Shop – including everything from salad onions to rainbow-hued Swiss chard, beans, basil, several varieties of tomato and cherry tomatoes, and Russian kale. Others sell in their

own farm shops, on roadside stalls or direct to hotels, pubs and restaurants. A handful of nurseries concentrates on herbs, again to supply specific customers in the catering sector. On the Isles of Scilly a cluster of growers, like Ruth and Paul Jenkins at Hillside Farm on Bryher, have recognized that they can supply visitors, local hotels, restaurants and pubs with herbs, vegetables and salad crops, partially filling a gap otherwise supplied by imported produce, and simultaneously boosting the quality of the eating experience that tourists are increasingly coming to expect.

One vegetable grown successfully on a small scale is asparagus. Cornwall has five sites where the wild variety grows, including the eponymous Asparagus Island off Kynance Cove, and a handful of commercial producers. John and Jenny Keeler at St Erme, near Truro, are the largest growers of this highly sought-after crop. During the brief season they sell at farmers' markets and to local restaurants. They also use a local wholesaler to distribute the succulent green spears across the county.

At the other end of the scale are large horticultural operations producing potatoes, cauliflowers, strawberries and spring greens. In addition to Cornish Earlies, main-crop potatoes are also big business in Cornwall – some farmers growing under contract for crisp manufacturers, others supplying the supermarkets. More than 6,000 acres of potatoes, 5,500 acres of broccoli (cauliflower), and 2,500 acres of spring greens are grown each year.

£2.80

PER

1 LB BUNDLE
(454g)

ASPARAGUS

Fresh cornish Asparagus

ASPARAGUS IS INCREDIBLY
HEALTHY AND TASTY

• Low in Calories
• Rich in Vitamins A, B6 and C
• Excellent source of Folic Acid
• Traditionally served with Hollandaise
  Sauce or Vinaigrette or dollop of Melting

Storage

Some of the best
strawberries in the world?
*Above:* Phil Boddington
checks the crop.
*Right:* Lithuanian student Jovita
Raubait samples the fruit.

Swede production is also expanding, to supply the thriving
Cornish pasty trade; other field-scale crops grown include
lettuce, carrots, onions and soft fruits. Horticulture is still big
business in Cornwall and, in monetary value, is the county's
third largest farming sector.

Strawberries, of course, are not exclusive to the Tamar Valley,
and have been grown in other parts of Cornwall for over 200
years. The red berry is still widely cultivated cross the county on
a significant scale. Some growers sell direct to the supermarkets,
others supply local markets or run pick-your-own operations.

One of the most innovative is Phil Boddington, situated in
the aptly named Avalon Gardens on slopes overlooking the sea
above Mevagissey. His family has been producing strawberries
for over 60 years, and has adapted the latest varietals and growing techniques to extend the season from April to November
– this includes using tables in polytunnels as well as outdoor
field cropping. What started as a mixed horticultural operation
has become one of Cornwall's biggest growers and the only
business concentrating solely on strawberries, supplying supermarkets, wholesalers, local shops, hotels, pubs and restaurants
and running a pick-your-own option. In addition to growing
top-class fruit, Phil and his wife Louise have branched out into
other strawberry products such as strawberry conserves (made
by hand in small batches perfect for cream teas), strawberry
vinegars, wine, liqueurs and syrups.

Phil Boddington believes it is the maritime growing conditions that put Cornish strawberries among the market leaders:
'Cornwall has the perfect climate to grow the best strawberries
in the world. The fruit ripens more slowly compared with, say,
the Vale of Evesham or Kent, increasing the sugar content so we
can get a much better and more intense flavour,' he said.

I think he is right – up to a point. I admire growers who have
adapted varieties and techniques to meet market demands for
year-round supplies of fresh fruit and vegetables as substitutes
for tasteless, under-ripe produce developed for its long shelf-
life, and its ability to travel thousands of food miles. But to me the best fruit and
vegetables are seasonal, special because they are only available at certain times of
year and for a short season – Tamar Valley strawberries, Cornish Earlies and asparagus being the perfect examples.

# strawberry gazpacho with pink and black peppercorn tuille biscuit

This strawberry soup is a novel way of serving strawberries – but as a dessert rather than at the start of the meal. The recipe comes from Richard O'Shea at the Cornish Range in Mousehole, where chefs Chad James and Joe Wardell are cooking up a storm using wonderful fresh fish and local ingredients. Richard, a local man, believes in cashing in on the abundance of excellent ingredients to be found within a few miles of this restaurant with rooms, which is tucked away in the far western reaches of the county.

## ingredients

*Serves 2–3*

For the gazpacho
- 200 g Cornish straw-berries
- juice of 1 orange
- Juice of 1 lime
- handful of mint leaves, finely chopped
- 3 basil leaves per serving, finely chopped
- sprig of mint
- crushed ice
- vanilla pod

For the biscuits
- 100 g icing sugar
- 75 g softened butter
- 50 ml egg whites
- 120 g plain flour
- cracked pink and black peppercorns
- brown sugar

- Cornish clotted cream to garnish

## method

*Tuille biscuits:* Liquidize softened butter and icing sugar together. Add plain flour and egg whites. Leave to stand for 20–25 minutes.

Smooth on to a baking tray to a thickness of 2 mm (or a baking tray lined with greaseproof paper or baking parchment). Sprinkle with brown sugar and cracked pink and black peppercorns.

Bake in a hot oven (200°C or gas 6) for four or five minutes, until golden brown.

*Strawberry gazpacho:* Squeeze orange and lime juice, and add to diced strawberries and seeds scraped from the vanilla pod.

Liquidize until smooth, add chopped mint and basil, and a little crushed ice.

Garnish with clotted cream, sprig of mint and tuille biscuit.

*Note:* Either serve immediately, or leave in the fridge to cool, in which case do not add the crushed ice until just before serving, otherwise the gazpacho will be too diluted.

*Top:* Chef Joe Wardell.
*Above:* The Cornish Range, Mousehole.

# 12 orchard fruits

The South West has a glorious orchard tradition. What is more evocative of spring than the sight of an apple orchard in full bloom, the blossoms swaying gently in the breeze? Although Somerset and Devon probably have the best known and most extensive apple orchards, despite having lost 40 per cent and 90 per cent respectively since 1950, Cornwall has an equally longstanding orchard tradition and lost a significant proportion of its orchards during the same time.

Celia Fiennes, travelling through the South West in the seventeenth century, noted that apples were frequently served to visitors. In 1698, while staying at the White Hart Inn in St Austell, she ate apple pie served with clotted cream, which she described as 'the most acceptable entertainment that could be made for me'.

Some horticulturists claim that Cornwall's damp, maritime climate and salt-laden winds are not conducive to apple growing, arguing that these conditions encourage mildew, canker and scab. Yet by the end of the eighteenth century the Tamar Valley orchards had a proven economic, as well as landscape value, providing cider for the Navy, based in Devonport at the mouth of the Tamar River.

Later, in Victorian times, Trelissick, on the Roseland peninsula, not far from Truro, and now run by the National Trust, was known as the 'fruit garden of Cornwall'. Further north in the Tamar Valley, James Lawry was encouraging significant planting of 'modern' apple trees and introduced Victoria plums for commercial production. Other extensive fruit-growing areas were probably the sheltered valleys of the Helford, Fowey, Fal, Camel and Hayle rivers.

John Harris, Head Gardener on the privately owned estate at Tresillian, four miles from the North Cornish coast, is living proof of the argument that apples, not to mention other top fruit, can be grown in Cornwall. In winter, he said, when an on-shore, north-westerly gale is blowing, 'you can taste the salt in the air';

*Right:* Apple blossom at Tresillian.
*Pages 168–9:* John Harris, in the old Cornish apple orchard at Tresillian.

*Above:* Traditional apple varieties: Pear Apple (*left*) and Rough Pippin (*right*). *Below:* The new Cornish orchard at Tresillian. *Right:* Label at Heligan.

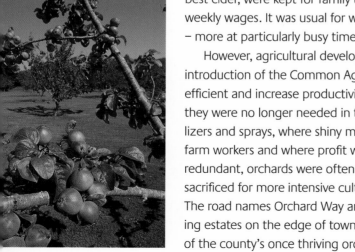

yet he has two thriving orchards. One was replanted in the winter of 1993–4 with over 80 Cornish apple varieties as part of the Cornish Orchards Project, the other has apples, pears, plums, cherries, medlars, quinces and mulberries. The oldest apple, the Tresillian Seedling, dates from 1504, and has been grown on the estate for 500 years. Other trees have evocative names – Strawberry Pippin, the earliest to be harvested each summer, and Cornish Longkeeper, a late-ripening apple which, as its names suggests, keeps until April or May the following year.

Until the middle of the twentieth century, most of the county's traditional, family-owned and run farms would have had a small orchard of apples, pears and other top fruit. The apples were usually used for cooking, eating and cider-making. Cider would have been made on every farm: the best apples, and the best cider, were kept for family use and the rest were part of the farm labourers' weekly wages. It was usual for workers to drink three or four pints of cider a day – more at particularly busy times such as the harvest.

However, agricultural development after the Second World War and the introduction of the Common Agricultural Policy forced farmers to become more efficient and increase productivity. Orchards lost their importance and relevance: they were no longer needed in the brave new world of artificial, chemical ferti-lizers and sprays, where shiny modern farm machinery replaced generations of farm workers and where profit was more important than pleasure. Unloved and redundant, orchards were often the first part of the farm to be grubbed up and sacrificed for more intensive cultivation, or the land was sold for development. The road names Orchard Way and Conference Close in the plethora of new hous-ing estates on the edge of towns and villages offer a clue to the demise of many of the county's once thriving orchards.

The Tamar Valley continued to be productive, for apples, cherries and also for its thriving market garden industry (see Chapter 11), which had developed in the late 1800s. The decline of market gardening coincided with the gradual abandonment and dereliction of many of the orchards, which would have disappeared altogether without the enthusiasm and hard work of Mary Martin and James Evans. Since the late 1970s the pair have recorded and revived the river valley's traditional fruit trees, tracking down and propagating more than 250 varieties of dessert, culinary and cider apples, cherries, plums and pears still growing in the county. They have catalogued 64 different Cornish apple varieties, including Cornish Gillyflower, Onion Redstreak, Colloggett Pippin, Manaccan Primrose and Plympton Pippin, and recorded the history of the orchards and market gardening.

## apple varieties

This list includes most of the Cornish varieties of apple, or varieties found growing in Cornwall that may have originated elsewhere. Some names and spellings may vary in different parts of the county and I make no claims to having a fully comprehensive list: the aim is to give a flavour of the rich diversity of apples that once grew in Cornwall's orchards for cider and culinary use. It has been compiled from a number of sources with the help of James Evans, Mary Martin and John Harris.

- Ben's Red
- Blackmoor Pippin
- Blackrock
- Bottlestopper
- Box Apple
- Breadfruit
- Captain Broad
- Cat's Head
- Chacewater Long-stem
- Colloggett Pippin (also known as Cornish Giant)
- Coombe Rough Cooker
- Cornish Aromatic
- Cornish Garden
- Cornish Gillyflower
- Cornish Honeypin
- Cornish Longstem
- Cornish Mother
- Cornish Pine

- Cornish Spice
- Cornish Wine Apple
- Crimson Bramley
- Devon Crimson Queen
- Duke of Cornwall
- Early Bower
- Fairfield
- Grow-bi-nights
- Gulval Seedling
- Hamlyn
- Hocking's Green
- Hocking's Yellow
- Hodge's Seedling
- Improved Keswick
- Jimmy Oliver
- John Standish
- John's Delight
- John's Early Eater
- King Byerd
- Lady's Fingers

- Lawry's No. 1 (Lord Grosvenor)
- Lizzy
- Longkeeper
- Lord of the Isles
- Magna Bonnum
- Manaccan Primrose
- Miel d'Or
- Onion Redstreak
- Pascoe's Pippin
- Pear Apple
- Pendragon
- Pig's Nose
- Pig's Snout
- Pitcher
- Plympton Pippin
- Polly Whitehair
- Queenie
- The Rattler
- Red Rollo
- Redstreak

- St James' Pippin
- Sawpit
- Scilly Pearl
- Sidney Strake
- Snell's Glass Apple
- Spiced Pippin
- Strawberry Pippin
- Sweet Larks
- Sweet Merlin
- Tan Harvey
- Tommy Knight
- Tregonna King
- Trenance Cooker
- Tresillian Seedling
- Turnip
- Veitch's Perfection
- Venus Pippin
- White Quarantine
- Wintergreen

Their work has proved that apples played as significant a role in Cornwall as anywhere else in the South West. The number of specifically Cornish apples suggests that the county's relative isolation encouraged the retention of varieties unique to individual areas and with very specific climatic conditions.

Work like this demonstrates the importance of local varieties and shows how modern apple cultivars, bred for uniformity, and easy growing and harvesting, survive in only the most anodyne and least demanding of growing conditions – gentle landscapes with a benign climate. Experts such as Mary Martin, James Evans and John Harris would readily admit that many of the indigenous varieties are often poor in appearance, hard, or disappointing to taste. But these characteristics developed for a reason, either for better keeping properties or hardiness to withstand difficult local conditions.

Sadly not all of these Cornish apples have survived, and only a handful – usually the best juicing or eating varieties – are in use. To ensure their continuity Mary and James have worked with the National Trust to create a mother orchard at Cotehele, to preserve all the Cornish top fruit varieties. Further south at Trelissick, the National Trust has recreated another Cornish fruit orchard, growing local apples, pears, plums and cherries.

While the county has few commercial orchards, many privately owned orchards have sprung back to life thanks to the work of the Cornish Orchards Project, which

*Above:* Andy Atkinson.
*Below:* Harvesting apples at Westnorth Manor Farm.
*Top right:* Pressing apples.
*Mid right:* Pasteurizing apple juice at Westnorth Manor Farm.
*Bottom right:* St Cuby's sparkling cider.

was run by Cornwall County Council during the 1990s. During the project's lifetime more than 3,000 new apple trees, all traditional Cornish varieties, were planted either in new orchards or to replace, reinvigorate and extend existing orchards, mostly in private ownership. In the Tamar Valley another orchard project, run by the Tamar Valley Area of Outstanding Natural Beauty team, is encouraging private owners to restore and replant orchards to keep local traditions alive.

There are still sufficient apples grown in Cornwall to supply a handful of businesses making apple juice and cider. New entrepreneurs are making apple juices and drinks alongside the few remaining, long-established cidermakers. As the bigger businesses are unable to rely entirely on Cornish, or their own, apples, supplies are topped up from trees planted during the Cornish Orchards Project, that are now fruiting, and from other West Country orchards.

Growers have recognized the value of growing traditional Cornish apple varieties. Jed and Sarah Trewhella, on the Helford River in West Cornwall, and Andy Atkinson, in the South East, are replanting Cornish varieties such as Manaccan Primrose, Chacewater Longstem, Scilly Pearl and Trenance Cooker. A trip to Westnorth Manor Farm, just outside Duloe in South East Cornwall, will not disappoint anyone looking for further proof that the Cornish apple industry, albeit small in scale, is thriving. Andy Atkinson is an apple enthusiast: there is nothing he likes better than to talk to visitors and fellow enthusiasts about his orchards, his apples, the process of making cider and apple juice, and his latest product, St Cuby's, a French-style, bottle-fermented, sparkling cider. His 260-acre farm was once run as a mixed livestock farm with mainly dairy cows and sheep. Now the animals have gone, apart from sheep occasionally brought in to graze the orchards. Westnorth Manor Farm is wholly devoted to apples, apple juice and cider, a direct result of Andy's decision to restore the farm's traditional orchard, which had been grubbed up years before. Replanting with traditional Cornish cider, eating and cooking apples started in 1993. In 1999, faced with his first full apple crop and realizing that this was more than one family could reasonably be expected to consume, Andy turned to apple juice and then cider-making. Each year he creates up to nine different apple juices and several varieties of cider, from farmhouse to bottle-fermented, sparkling cider. His solution became his salvation: what started as a small diversification has become the farm's main source of income.

*Top:* At Westnorth Manor Farm, cider is stored in oak barrels.
*Above:* Andy Atkinson's Cornish Farmhouse Cider.

The hard work starts in late summer as the first apples are picked – some on the farm, and others on neighbouring farms and from orchards across the county. After washing and sorting, the apples pass through a mill which macerates them, forcing them out on to a cloth where they are piled up several centimetres deep. Seven or eight of these form the cheese which is then slowly, hydraulically pressed until it is no more than a centimetre deep. The juice runs off and goes straight to the bottling tank, where vitamin C is added (the only addition during the entire process), to ensure a long life. The remaining pomace is fed to cows on a neighbouring farm.

Once bottled the juice is pasteurized. Andy believes that this method helps retain the full depth of flavour in the bottle. The simple process creates a pure, unadulterated product that ranges in style from fresh and fruity – the early pressings – to rich and mellow juices, made from apples ripening later in the season.

Within those ranges, specific apple varieties are used – such as Cornish Gillyflower or Grenadier – which give each juice its individual characteristics. Andy normally uses a mix of culinary, dessert and cider apples and then blends the juice until he has achieved the correct balance, each juice having what he calls a complicated style with plenty of depth and flavour.

Just as apple juice production finishes, cider-making begins. Dessert and culinary apples used for juices need to be processed within a very short time of being picked. Fortunately for cidermakers, cider apples are less exacting. They benefit from being heaped up and left to mature, giving the natural starches time to be converted into sugars. So while the juice is being made the cider apples sit waiting and maturing.

The same pressing process is repeated and then the resulting juice is either piped into oak barrels – often recycled from whisky or brandy distilleries, which give particular flavours to the cider – or stainless steel vats, used for making St Veryan cider, a stronger drink. Andy can eulogize for hours on the alchemy of cider-making – the chemistry that turns 'a base material into something golden and wonderful'.

By January all the fruit has been converted into juice or cider, has been bottled or is maturing quietly in barrels and vats. The activity of the late summer and autumn months has died away for another year, but there is plenty of work still to do and plenty of fresh, tangy apple juice waiting for eager buyers.

Like any dedicated artisan food producer, Andy Atkinson is a great believer in the effects of *terroir* on the flavour and qualities of his product, so lucky visitors to Westnorth Manor Farm can linger in his tasting shop and discover for them-selves the mixture of flavours, sharp and sweet, soft and fruity, that characterize his products. As his business expands he is constantly looking for new sources of apples and buys from growers as far away as Bristol. In many cases his decision to buy guarantees the future of another West Country orchard, maintaining  the wonderful landscape features that would otherwise wither away and die.

# plums and cherries

Apples are not the only tree-fruit with a long history in Cornwall. In his 1602 *Survey of Cornwall* Richard Carew noted that the most prosperous landowners had access to the same range of fruits as elsewhere in England:

> Pears, plums, pear-plums, cherries, mulberries, chestnuts and walnuts,
> ... the gentlemen step not far behind those of other parts.

After apples, the Kea plum stands out as the fruit with an essentially Cornish identity. Although it is no longer grown commercially, small pockets of this plum remain – a few in private orchards, some growing wild around Coombe creek and in the Kea parishes bordering the Fal estuary between Truro and Falmouth, and some replanted by enthusiasts such as John Harris at Tresillian, who believes that there were up to 20 distinctive West Country plums. He grows 12 different plums including six Cornish varieties: Manaccan, Wadebridge, Bodmin and Truro plums, Golden Kea and Black Kea. The rest probably died out due to lack of demand. Small quantities of Kea Plum Wine™ are made by Polmassick vineyard (see Chapter 13);

*Above:* Kea plums.

otherwise, Kea plums tend to be used for jam and preserves. The sour, deep purple fruits, similar to a damson, are difficult to eat raw and have a relatively short shelf-life, another factor that may have led to their decline.

Plums are not the only orchard fruit struggling to survive in Cornwall. The Tamar Valley, once the most productive part of Cornwall for its fruit, flowers and vegetables, and particularly famed for its sweet, dark, almost black cherries, has few productive cherry trees left. A handful still grow wild in hedges and on the river banks, just as they did 200 years ago before being cultivated for commercial use. A few remnants survive in private ownership, and some new orchards have been planted in Botus Fleming and nearby St Dominick. The original cherry orchards grew fruit that was less prone to being attacked by the birds and more resistant to splitting, compared with fruit grown in Kent. Almost all these cherries were sold locally, such was their fame and popularity.

It is hard to believe that when cherry production was at its height, blossom-time boat trips went up the river from Plymouth to see the trees as they flowered, and at harvest time cherry-pie picnics were commonplace. Sadly for the landscape, the new trees will be modern, easier to manage and pick than the older, 60–65 ft trees, which needed 40- or 50-rung ladders to ensure thorough picking. Somehow I doubt that they will have the same visual impact – tall, knarled trunks supporting a canopy of delicate, white blossom swaying in the breeze – but at least the tradition is kept alive.

*Below:* Site of the old cherry orchards on the banks of the River Tamar.
*Right:* An old Kea plum orchard in Coombe creek.

This recipe, using cider as the natural partner to pork, comes from Langmans Restaurant in Callington. Owned by Anton and Gail Buttery, it was Cornwall Tourist Board's Restaurant of the Year in 2002 and 2004, and runner-up in 2003. The Butterys serve top quality Cornish cuisine, using local produce wherever possible. Anton often puts a modern twist on Cornish classics. This recipe needs specific seasonal produce, and uses pork from Sally Lugg's Primrose Herd rare breed pigs, from near Redruth.

# roast loin of pork, cider and whole-grain mustard sauce, shallots and cider, cornish asparagus and cornish earlies

## ingredients

*Serves 4*

Cider shallots
- 400 g shallots
- 500 ml cider
- 3 tbsps cider vinegar
- 1 tbsp sugar
- sea salt, freshly ground black pepper

Roast loin of pork
- 500 g loin from a black pig, well trimmed of all skin and fat, and tied in a roll

- 250 g baby spinach, washed
- 200 g oyster mushrooms

Cider and whole-grain mustard sauce
- 500 ml Cornish Orchards cider
- 250 ml chicken stock
- 1 tbsp cider vinegar
- 1 tbsp whole-grain mustard
- 75 g unsalted butter
- sea salt, freshly ground black pepper
- Cornish Early potatoes
- Cornish asparagus

## method

*Cider shallots:* Peel and finely chop the shallots. Put them in a pan and add the rest of the ingredients. Bring to the boil with the lid on, and simmer for 30 minutes. Remove the lid and carry on cooking until there is no liquid left.

*Roast loin of pork:* Remove the skin and reserve it for crackling. Lay it out and remove as much fat as possible. Cut it into strips about 1/2 cm x 12 cm. Place it on a baking tray covered with baking parchment, and sprinkle with flaked sea salt. Cover with more baking parchment and place another tray on top. Put into preheated oven at 180°C (gas 4) for around 30 minutes, or until crisp. Tie the pork in a roll, and season with salt and pepper. Place in a hot pan with oil; sear the pork until lightly browned, remove and place it on a tray. Put in a pre-heated oven at 180°C (gas 4). Roast for about 20 minutes, or until just cooked but still slightly pink. Remove, cover and allow to rest for 10–15 minutes. Meanwhile, sauté the oyster mushrooms in butter with seasoning, and wilt the spinach in a little butter.

*Top:* Anton Buttery.
*Above:* Langmans Restaurant, Callington.

*Cider and whole-grain mustard sauce:* Pour the Cornish Orchards cider, chicken stock and cider vinegar into a pan; bring to the boil, then simmer to reduce to 250 ml. Blend in the butter until it is all incorporated and keep it warm. Just before serving, whisk in the whole-grain mustard and season to taste.

*To serve:* Place a mound of spinach in the centre of a plate, topped with oyster mushrooms. Remove the string from the pork and carve. Lay four or five slices on the mushrooms; top with a quenelle of cider shallots, and finish with a stick of crackling. Pour sauce around. Serve with Cornish Earlies and Cornish asparagus or other seasonal vegetables.

# 13 vines and wines

If there is one place in Cornwall that illustrates clearly how farming has shaped the landscape and the impact each has on the other, it is the Isles of Scilly. Food production on this group of over 100 islands, 28 miles from Lands End, has never been easy. The highest point on the islands is about 150 ft, and they are exposed to damp, salty winds rushing in from the Atlantic, particularly in the winter. Looking west from St Agnes or Bryher there is nothing but sea between the islands and the eastern seaboard of America. At the same time the islands benefit from a mild, warm climate, which gives the farmers and growers a two or three-week advantage over mainland Cornwall. Frosts are extremely rare – the average winter temperature is 5°C – but when they do occur they can be devastating to the subtropical plants that grow luxuriantly in the islands' gardens and countryside.

For hundreds of years farming and food production on the islands was basic and rudimentary – most families depended on fish, shellfish, seaweed and what they could grow themselves. The thin, poor soil was difficult to cultivate as the salt-laden winter winds covered fields and crops with sand and sea-spray.

Although during the nineteenth century mainland farming was modernizing, significant change on the Isles of Scilly was not so obvious, given the size of the islands and their distance from potential new markets. Feeding the islanders continued to take priority. But in the 1820s the harvest failed, and potatoes, which had been successfully exported for many years, were becoming less profitable. Things only improved in 1883, when Algernon Dorrien-Smith, lessee of the Tresco estate, used imported bulbs to encourage the Tresco growers to cultivate narcissi for the Covent Garden flower market. For more than 120 years flower-growing has been Scillonian farmers' main source of income. Soleil d'Ors and Paper Whites (the earliest narcissi) are exported, while most of the islanders' food is imported.

*Right:* Grapes at Camel Valley Vineyard.

However, the combination of increasing freight costs and competition from other countries has gradually eroded the profitability of flower-growing, making it far less extensive than 50 years ago. The islands' appearance has changed rapidly and dramatically: many of the tiny flower fields are overgrown by wild flowers, brambles and bracken, which also threaten to invade the other uncultivated areas.

One woman who was not prepared to abandon her family farm is Val Thomas, whose family has grown flowers on St Martin's (one of the five inhabited islands) for several generations. Although the farm is only a few yards from the sea and just 60 ft at its highest point, the former teacher and her husband Graham have planted the most south-westerly vineyard in Britain.

In 1996 Reichensteiner vines were planted on tiny, gently sloping south-facing fields, enclosed by shelter-belts of escallonia, pittosporum and veronica. A total of five acres have since been planted with a mix of other varieties to make white, red and sparkling wine. Val Thomas is clearly determined to minimize the difficulties of growing grapes in such an exposed location, and to keep this part of Scilly under cultivation and not allow it to revert to wilderness. The first tiny grape crop was harvested in 1999, but the first vintage to be sold was the millennium vintage the following year.

If the St Martin's Vineyard is one of the newest in Cornwall, it has strong historical precedents. Cornish wine is not the anachronism it may seem, although it

Reichensteiner vines on St Martin's, Isles of Scilly.

would be fair to say that Cornish viticulture, just like the English wine industry, is likely to remain a niche activity unless global warming makes a significant climatic impact.

Vitis vinifera – the type of grape grown in all modern wine-producing areas – is not native to Britain, but was probably imported by the Romans, who introduced wine-drinking to Britain and northern Europe. The conquering Romans moved quite a long way west, but their cultural influence was barely felt west of Exeter, and in Cornwall the presence was largely military – a fort was built at Nanstallon on the River Camel. There is evidence that tin and other precious metals were sold at trading posts such as at Probus. When the Anglo-Saxons succeeded the Romans, the Celts retreated into Wales and Cornwall, and largely ignored Anglo-Saxon ways. It was not until the Norman invasion that new influences took hold, including grape-growing and wine production. Although in 1086 the 'Domesday Book' mentioned 46 vineyards, none were in Cornwall and the furthest west appears to have been at North Curry, near Taunton. However, that does not rule out the possibility of Cornish vineyards at that time, and by 1259 records show that vines were grown at Gear and Halnoweth in St Martin in Meneage, on the Lizard.

After the Normans the nobility and the Church continued cultivating vines and making wine with some seriousness, but in Cornwall it remained a minority activity, even among the county's landowners. Richard Carew noted, in his *Survey of Cornwall*, that while grapes apparently grew well, there was little evidence of vinification:

Yet one special privilege which the nearness to the south, the fitness of the grounds standing upon limestones, the well growing of vines and the pleasant taste of their grapes do seem to grant, I have not hitherto known by any to be put in practice, and that is the making of wines.

*Top:* Val Thomas inspects new growth on the vines. *Above*: A bottle of St Martin's Vineyard wine. *Below:* Wine tasting at St Martin's Vineyard.

The dissolution of the monasteries in 1536–40 and climate change in the seventeenth century are often cited as the two factors that caused the demise of English wine-making, but there is plenty of evidence showing that it continued, on a small scale, until early in the twentieth century. It is true that after the dissolution of the monasteries it

declined, probably more because of the difficulties of making good wine – in the face of easy access to imported wines – and a general disaffection with the whole process, but it did not die out completely. James I had his own vineyard in Surrey; the diarist Samuel Pepys refers frequently to drinking wine made by his hosts, and in 1611 Robert Cecil, the first Earl of Salisbury, planted more than 30,000 vines at Hatfield House.

English wine-making continued with this mix of nobility, eccentricity, private and horticultural interest until it was effectively brought to an end by sugar short-ages during the First World War. It was only in the last 30 years of the twentieth century that English viticulture re-emerged as an activity to be taken seriously, building on the work of Ray Barrington Brock, and pioneers such as Sir Guy Salisbury-Jones and Gillian Pearkes, who set out to re-establish grape-growing in the post-war years.

Polmassick, near Mevagissey in South East Cornwall, was the county's first commercial vineyard, planted in 1978. Barbara Musgrave has been vigneron, winemaker and licensee since 1986, cultivating 2.5 acres of vines – double the number planted when she and her husband arrived there. While she admits that the vineyard does not make her a large living each year, neither is production so poor that she has to give up – a roundabout way of saying that she is probably quite comfortable with the current arrangements, selling virtually all she produces at the vineyard gate, with a small amount sold through local shops.

Like other Cornish vineyards, the steeply sloping fields above the Luney valley face south or south-west. This is the kind of landscape best suited to growing grapes – the vines like heat, good drainage and plenty of sun, although some recent hybrid varieties have been bred so that the grapes will ripen without large amounts of direct sunshine. Although sheltered, the area is still prone to frost. Like most other new vineyard owners, Barbara Musgrave grows modern hybrids, whose names are unfamiliar to wine-buyers accustomed to Cabernet Sauvignon, Merlot and Chardonnay.

One of the most interesting wines, because of its inherent Cornishness, is Polmassick Kea Plum Wine™, made from the old Cornish plum variety (see Chapter 12) once grown widely in the coombs and valleys around the Fal estuary and Truro. Although the fruit is rare compared with 100 years ago, Barbara Musgrave always manages to find sufficient Kea plums to make this red, fruity dessert wine which is blended with her own Pinot Noir to produce an interesting mix of plum and spice flavours – a light wine, with a dry finish and a hefty 12.5% ABV, which is delicious served chilled as an aperitif or with summer fruits.

Perhaps one reason why Cornwall is not more prominent as a wine-making county is that it is more vulnerable to damp winds than other parts of the south-

*Above:* Kea Plum Wine™ is one of the most interesting Cornish wines.
*Right:* The Camel Valley Vineyard.

west peninsula, which can be crucial when the vines flower. Nevertheless, Bob Lindo, at Camel Valley Vineyard, has gone a long way towards demonstrating that Cornish wine-making can be a successful commercial activity.

Nationally and internationally he is regarded as 'a phenomenon on the English wine scene', making excellent wines that are taken seriously in the national and international wine world where they score highly in blind tastings, and have won several prestigious awards. If anyone has contributed to the change in approach to Cornish wines it is Bob Lindo, who has invigorated the industry with a pro-fessionalism that most would acknowledge was missing from the English wine industry as recently as 1980.

Situated above the Camel Valley, between Wadebridge and Bodmin, Bob describes his 10-acre vineyard, first planted in 1986, as combining 'traditional vineyard practices' with 'a New World approach to wine-making'.

Attention to detail and the right equipment are critical, he believes, and the investment in machinery at Camel Valley is impressive, making it probably the most modern-equipped vineyard and winery in the country.

The south-facing slopes above the Camel River are ideal for vine growing – the clear Cornish air, warm, mild climate and long summer days contribute to Camel Valley's distinctive styles of wine. By selecting a range of vines suited to northern climates, the vineyard can produce up to nine different wines ranging from dry white to red, rosé, sparkling wine and a pink sparkling wine, depending on the vintage. In some vintages a sweet white wine is also made.

The first tiny, 200-bottle vintage was made in 1991. More than a decade later the vineyard is booming: in one month in 2003 Camel Valley sold more than 70,000 bottles of wine, although it is important to understand that while vintages like 2003 can be outstanding, in other years – 1993, for example – no wine is made at all.

*Left:* Harvesting grapes at Camel Valley Vineyard.
*Above:* Bob Lindo.
*Below:* Crushing the grapes.

Like many other Cornish vignerons, Bob Lindo has elected not to use the grape varietal names on many of his wines 'as they sound too foreign'. 'At-lantic Dry has an immediate association with the area,' he said. 'Provenance is everything, and that is where Cornwall has a huge advantage.'

Bob's success is tinged with a healthy dose of realism. He warned that making wine in England is always a risky busi-ness, needing more than just enthusiasm and dedication. It requires commitment,

patience and considerable investment before there is any return. 'You
need to be able to afford to lose
money – we certainly didn't make
any money for several years,' he said.

If Bob Lindo at Camel Valley has
put Cornish wine on the map, giving it
a market presence from which other
Cornish vineyards benefit, the smaller
boutique vineyards seem content to
work at a slower pace, although they
share the same attitude to growing
grapes and making wine.

Paul Sibley at Bosue, who combines grapes with growing flowers
and foliage, and working away from his farm, is joining
forces with another relative newcomer, Graham Sher-
ratt, who is building a new state-of-the-art winery.
While perhaps not expecting to make a fortune from
his three acres of vines, Paul Sibley is another example
of the new, professional approach, making modern
styles of wines.

As recently as 1980 English wine-making was
mostly the preserve of either eccentric enthusiasts or
retired military types who could live comfortably on
their pensions without needing their vineyards to be
profitable. Since then the face of English wine-making
has changed: different varieties of grapes are grown,
the (mostly New World) flying winemakers have
introduced new styles of wine and, arguably, global
warming is making it easier to produce better quality
wines more consistently.

Let's put this into perspective. Cornwall's six commercial vineyards grow 22 acres of vines. The English
wine industry, with 400 vineyards in England and
Wales covering 2,000 acres, produces between three
and five million bottles of wine a year, depending on
the year. Cornwall might produce 1 per cent of that.
In a global context, in 1998 France produced 52.6

## vines and grapes

Although the grape vine, *Vitis vinifera*,
is not native to the UK, since the 1950s
English growers have been successful
with a variety of grapes. Most started with
types already grown on the Continent,
such as Muller Thurgau, but more
recently they have started planting
modern hybrids better suited to northern
European climates and soils, such as
Seyval Blanc or Orion. Varieties grown in
Cornwall are:

- Bacchus
- Dornfelder
- Findling
- Kernling
- Madeleine Angevine
- Muller Thurgau
- Orion
- Ortega
- Phoenix
- Pinot Noir
- Regent
- Reichensteiner
- Rondo
- Seyval Blanc

million hectolitres of wine, whereas English vineyards produced 12,000 hectolitres of wine.

For those really committed to their vineyards it is clear that in Cornwall making wine can and does work. Although Cornish wine-making will always remain a niche activity, the products are top quality, stylish, drink well, and cannot be ignored. Fortunate vineyard visitors have the benefit of tasting excellent wines in beautiful settings.

More than one of the vineyard owners I met reminded me of the old adage 'to make a small fortune from wine you need to start with a large one'. With uncertain harvests, and perhaps not always ideal climatic conditions, Cornish winemakers are a dedicated band who deserve to succeed.

*Left:* Stalks after crushing grapes.
*Above:* Cheers! Lunchtime at Camel Valley Vineyard.
*Below:* Bottles of sparkling wine at Camel Valley.

# rick stein's white wine syllabub

This recipe comes from Rick Stein, of Padstow's Seafood Restaurant. It is taken from *Rick Stein's Food Heroes: Another Helping* (BBC Books, 2004), in which he features some of the best food and drink to be found in Britain. Cornwall is prominent in this collection.

Rick Stein hardly needs an introduction, and is to be commended for almost single-handedly starting the renaissance of Cornish food with the opening of the Seafood Restaurant in 1978. Since then his food empire in Padstow, North Cornwall, has expanded to include a café, bistro, cookery school, delicatessen, patisserie and his most recent venture, a fish and chip shop. While not using Cornish produce exclusively, Rick Stein is passionate about high quality, speciality producers – his food heroes – and their products. Many Cornish food producers feature in his two books on the subject.

## ingredients

For this recipe Rick Stein recommends using Bacchus, made by Bob Lindo at Camel Valley Vineyard.

*Serves 6*
- finely grated zest and juice of one large lemon
- 2 tbsps brandy
- 50 g caster or icing sugar
- 150 ml medium-dry, spicy white wine
- 300 ml double cream
- sponge fingers to serve

*Top:* Rick Stein.
*Above:* Camel Valley Bacchus.
*Left:* Recipe prepared for *Gourmet Cornwall* by Gerry Boriosi and Emma Hoskins at Cornwall College.

## method

Mix together the lemon zest and juice, brandy, sugar and white wine in a bowl. Cover and chill overnight, or for at least an hour.

Next day strain the wine mixture, discarding the lemon zest.

Put the cream in a bowl and whisk, slowly adding the wine mixture until the cream loosely holds its shape and leaves a ribbon on the surface when trailed from the whisk. Do not over whisk or it will curdle.

Spoon the syllabub into tall glasses or small cups, and leave somewhere cool until ready to serve. Decorate with a small twist of lemon peel if you wish. Serve with sponge fingers.

*Author's note:* Try serving with almond biscotti made by Linda Tonkin at Blue Mango in Truro.

# 14 cuckoos in eden

How do you fancy a Cornish Blonde, a trip round Lizard Point or a Speckled Parrot? Your Surf Boar will appear Dreckly with an Old Bustard perched on it. Fans of Cornish beers will recognize some of these distinctive names, and there are plenty more. Scuppered, Cornish Knocker, Spingo, Heligan Honey, Cornish Corgi and Eden Ale represent some of the Cornish brewpubs, microbreweries and breweries that produce a wide range of real ales in Cornwall and the Isles of Scilly. Only in Cornwall is such an apparently light-hearted approach taken to beer names, but which in fact reflect the county's history, folklore and modern obsessions. How much more interesting to drink a beer named after a tin-mine fairy (Cornish Knocker) than Stella or Bloggs Best Bitter?

Spingo is Cornwall's most legendary beer, brewed at the Blue Anchor in Helston, a historic, thatched building dating back to the 1400s, when it was a church house inn where the monks provided ale, food and probably lodging for travellers. After the dissolution of the monasteries it became a village tavern and later, during the eighteenth and nineteenth centuries when Helston was one of the Cornish tin-mining centres, it was frequented by many local miners. The Blue Anchor has survived to become one of the oldest breweries in the country, and is certainly the oldest in Cornwall. Ale, followed by beer, has probably been brewed there almost continuously for around 600 years. By the 1970s, when CAMRA started campaigning to revive real ales, it was one of England's four remaining pubs still brewing its own beer.

Spingo is the generic name for the pub's beers, derived from stingo, a Victorian word meaning strong beer, and they are notorious for their strength. The weakest in the range is IPA (also known as Jubilee) at 4.5 per cent ABV, with Ordinary Special at 6.5 per cent, and Easter or Christmas Special at 7.6 per cent.

*Right:* The Blue Anchor, Helston. *Pages 194–5:* Tim Sears brewing at The Blue Anchor.

It's not surprising that these beers are renowned for their side effects compared with the slightly lower ABV of most real ales. Could this be why one of Helston's taxi companies operates from immediately outside the pub?

The Blue Anchor has become something of an institution, more than just a pub, more than just a brewery, it is unique. People visit from all over the world because of the pub's long history and its inimitable beers. In 2001 Tim Sears, the brewer, developed Bragget to celebrate the 800th anniversary of Helston's charter. Regularly brewed since, it is a hopless ale based on original ale recipes, and uses apple juice to add sweetness and flavour.

In Cornwall, as elsewhere, the development of the county's public houses, commercial brewers and malthouses can be measured by the number of Brewery Lanes and The Maltings in Cornish towns and villages, often home to anonymous modern housing estates or new business parks with little real sense of the history and traditions behind the name. As we reach for a glass of beer, how many of us remember that it is one of Britain's oldest drinks, and was almost as important as bread in the Cornishman's daily diet? The development of one went hand-in-hand with the other, and the synergy between the two makes them almost indivisible: made from the same basic ingredients – grain, water and a fermenting agent – ale also contributed ale-barm as a raising agent for bread.

As with so much of our best food and drink, brewing may appear to be a simple process – in this case using only malted barley, water, hops and yeast – but it relies on far more than just a chemical reaction. Good real ale is the result of an alchemy that depends equally on the brewer's skills, the quality of the ingredients and the care, attention and dark arts of the cellarman.

In a time when we are willing to pay more for a litre of bottled water than for a pint of milk, it may be hard to believe that for hundreds of years beer was the safest thing to drink – water was not safe, but the process of brewing rendered it so. Except in the very poorest families, ale was drunk by every family member at every meal. Adults would have had stronger ales while servants and children would drink small (weaker) ales.

Ale was the drink of peasants, monks, working men and the nobility. Large establishments and small households brewed their own; taverns and village alehouses either made their own or were supplied by the local manor house; and later a few enterprising businesses started small-scale commercial breweries. Ale was made principally from grain and water, possibly with some honey added or other spices and herbs to disguise the flavour as it tended to deteriorate quickly, so it was sweeter than modern beers and ales.

Hopped beer, closer to modern beers and tasting less sweet, was introduced from Europe in the fifteenth century. The Flemish had discovered that adding hops not only made a drink with a sharper, bitter flavour, it also improved the keeping qualities. For a while beer and ale co-existed, despite Henry VIII's attempts to outlaw beer by banning the use of hops. But as beer's popularity increased it eventually displaced ale altogether, leaving some confusion as both names continued in use.

It is likely that at this time in Cornwall, Devon and Somerset as much cider would be consumed as beer. Cider-making had developed after the Norman Conquest and was popular, particularly in the south-west counties, where it later became part of farm workers' wages (see Chapter 12). Its popularity is perhaps not surprising if Cornish beer was as bad as contemporary writers, such as Andrew Boorde, claimed. In his 1542 book *Compenyous*

*Regyment, or A Dyetary of Helth*, the physician described Cornish beer as 'looking white and thick as [if] pigs had wrestled in it, smoky and ropy.'

At this time Cornish ale would have been made from either oats or barley, changing almost exclusively to barley as production increased in the sixteenth century. Later, to meet the growing taste for the new beer, hops were grown in many parts of Cornwall, including on the Roseland peninsula, around St Kew and Mevagissey. However, by the start of the nineteenth century, hops were declining in favour of other crops. All the current Cornish breweries use hops grown outside the county, and most use malted barley supplied by Tuckers Maltings, the only remaining traditional malthouse in the South West. There is a growing impetus to source locally grown barley, and wheat for wheat beers, wherever possible.

Ale, or beer, was more than just a drink. Along with the alehouse, and later pubs and beer houses, ale was at the heart of many social occasions, feasts, festivals and later fairs and agricultural shows. Richard Carew's 1602 *Survey of Cornwall* describes the tradition of church ales at around the same time, in which each parish elected two young men to be responsible for the church ale feast. Money was collected from each parishioner to be used to brew ales and buy the ingredients for a parish-wide celebration, usually held at Whitsuntide or other church holidays. Church ales were supposed to raise funds for the church and the needy in the parish, but in many parishes they fell into disrepute, gaining a reputation for encouraging drunkenness, lasciviousness and disorderly behaviour. These Whitsuntide feasts were the precursor for the tea treats, church feasts and other festivities (see Chapter 10).

By the eighteenth century – despite the influence of the Methodists John and Charles Wesley, who at one point had persuaded 64 per cent of the population that the chapel was

*Below:* Barley ripening near Penzance.

## smuggling, wrecks and wrecking

For hundreds of years, smuggling and wrecking were important activities that enhanced the quality of the food and drink consumed in Cornwall, and particularly on the Isles of Scilly which lay on the course of all the main trade routes from America, the Mediterranean, Africa and the East.

This book is not the place to discuss the issue of whether the Cornish were deliberate wreckers, but there is no doubt that the act of saving afflicted sailors gave poor working families access to precious cargoes such as meat, spices, fruit and spirits they could not otherwise have afforded. Often this would have unexpected consequences – there are several tales of entire villages turning out to rescue the crew and/or cargo from a wrecked ship but becoming so intoxicated by the alcohol on board that terrible accidents happened, in one case setting fire to the ship and losing not just the ship but the entire cargo and several lives.

Just as important was the smuggling trade, which gave entire communities, rich and poor, landowners and clergymen as well as working families, access to wine, brandy, rum, port, sherry, whisky (from Ireland), gin (known as Geneva), coffee, cocoa, chocolate, tea, sugar and salt (these last three all highly taxed in normal circumstances). Salt, of course, was vital for curing fish, and was a major smuggled item for hundreds of years, coming mostly from France.

Many Cornish recipes make bold use of these goods, particularly brandy, wine and other spirits, as these were difficult to conceal in any quantity for any length of time. The simplest solution was to use them.

There were well-established smuggling routes between Cornwall and the Channel Islands, Ireland France and Holland. In 1770 it is said that 470,000 gallons of brandy were smuggled into Cornwall – far more than was officially imported through the port of London the same year. A few years later a Polperro ship was caught off Lundy Island with a cargo of 6,632 lbs of tea, 2,224 gallons of brandy and 90 casks of gin. There are many reports of fighting and rowdiness breaking out at times when large quantities of alcohol were landed.

Although a Customs board was created in 1671, it was not until 1829 when the coastguard service was set up that smuggling came under some degree of control. Until then the Cornish viewed smuggling as free trade both in and out of the county, to avoid punitive taxes on imports and exports. It was a matter of pride in Cornish communities to be able to outwit the customs men, often their own relations. In many ports and harbours, such as Looe, some officials were not averse to receiving their share of the booty at a later date, or being bribed to turn a blind eye.

In place of smuggling Cornwall has recently acquired its own distillery. The Cornish Cyder Farm makes cider brandy and fruit-flavoured eau-de-vies distilled from its own cider or fruit wines. In partnership with the St Austell Brewery it has also distilled the first official Cornish whisky, using Cornish barley. The initial distillation is maturing in oak barrels, but is not expected to be ready for bottling before 2010.

the better place to worship – the consumption of beer and other alcohol had reached such levels that there was great concern about the damage to family life, morality and the social order. The mayhem caused by excessive drinking was also exacerbated by the easy availability of cheap smuggled spirits, particularly gin, rum and brandy. The Cornish were criticized for being an intemperate lot.

The miners particularly had gained a reputation for hard drinking, especially on and immediately after each month's pay day. Such was this culture of drunkenness and debauchery that the first working day after pay day became known as Mazed Monday, as frequently many of the men were still too mazed from the after effects of a weekend's hard drinking to be able to work underground.

In 1830 the Beer House Act was passed. It was intended to reduce the widespread consumption of liquor, legal and illegal, by raising taxes on gin and other spirits. Beer and cider would be promoted instead, at the same time helping farmers by increasing demand for barley and hops. The new law permitted any householder to get an excise licence to sell beer, and as a result hundreds of small beer houses or beer shops, known in Cornwall as 'kiddleywinks' or simply 'winks', appeared in every town, village and hamlet throughout the county. The Lamorna Inn, in West Cornwall, is still known locally as 'the wink'. Although officially licensed to sell only beer, in many remote areas the kiddleywinks also served smuggled brandy, gin, rum and other spirits. Inns continued to sell spirits and beer legally, and to offer board and lodging; there were also public houses, the new beer houses, bush houses – indicated by a bundle of furze over the door showing drink was available – and spirit shops. These last were distinguished from beer houses as they sold beer and liquor to be taken away, whereas beer sold in beer houses had to be consumed on the premises.

*Below and right:* Sharp's beers at the Royal Cornwall Show.

The new laws simply made the existing problem worse. In 1832 there were 29 public houses and beer shops in Bodmin; six years later there were 29 public houses and 37 beer shops in Penzance. Almost 30 years after that, in 1867, the *West Briton* reported how far the beer culture had flooded the county:

> Cornwall contains 688 public houses, 29 of which have been convicted of offences during the year; with 175 beer houses, 21 having been convicted. There are only two refreshment houses with wine licences within the county jurisdiction, and the number of tramp, or low lodging houses, does not exceed 42.

This only changed when the licensing system was altered in 1869, putting magistrates instead of excise officers in charge of issuing annual licences. From 1870 onwards the number of beer houses declined rapidly, yet more than 130 years later it is estimated that there are still more than 650 pubs in Cornwall. However, their

role has changed beyond recognition since the introduction of drink-driving laws, booze cruises and the dominance of the supermarkets as a convenient, one-stop shopping solution.

Although there had been small-scale brewers earning a living in Cornwall for hundreds of years, the Redruth Brewery (now closed) was the first commercial Cornish brewery of any scale, set up in 1742 on the back of the town's huge success as the world centre for copper mining. Other breweries have come and gone since, but Cornwall still has a wide range of real ale brewers of all shapes and sizes. These range from the St Austell Brewery – set up in 1851 and still run by direct descendants of its founder Walter Hicks – to newcomers like Skinners and Sharps, to a handful of tiny microbreweries and pub brewhouses. The Driftwood Spars at St Agnes, for example, brews just one beer, Cuckoo Ale, solely for consumption on the premises. Fourteen breweries of varying sizes make more than 60 beers, available either in pubs as guest beers or in local and national shops, supermarkets and off-licences. In addition to real ale, some make stout – including the Organic Brewhouse at Helston, Cornwall's only organic brewery. There are also barley wines, wheat beers, or occasional beers to celebrate specific occasions such as the Queen's Jubilee, Christmas or the 1999 total eclipse of the sun.

Britain's most southerly, and one of the newer Cornish microbreweries is Ales of Scilly, on St Mary's in the Isles of Scilly, 28 miles south-west of Land's End. It was set up by Mark Praeger in 1999 when he decided to give up teaching and earn a living from his lifelong hobby and passion. A true perfectionist, it took him two years to reach the point where he was happy to sell his first brew, Maiden Voyage. His brewing process usually takes a minimum of ten days from mash to drinking, although Mark Praeger prefers to allow longer cask conditioning where possible. It is hard to believe that at first he struggled to persuade the islanders that a real ale of their own was something worth having – testament to the power and influence of 40 years of the big breweries promoting keg beer and lagers. As he put it: 'There was no real tradition of real ale drinking on the islands. There were a lot of lager drinkers out there that had to be converted.'

*Below:* Mark Praeger and Ales of Scilly beer.
*Top right:* Local beers at The New Inn, Tresco.
*Bottom right:* The Mermaid Pub, St Mary's, Isles of Scilly.

The story has changed since then, and Mark Praeger finds it hard to keep up with demand for his two different ales, Scuppered and Natural Beauty – a lighter beer designed to appeal to summer visitors and reflecting the islands' status as an Area of Outstanding Natural Beauty. Like many of Cornwall's other real ale brewers, Mark also creates one-offs for special events, such as Joggered, for the Tresco marathon, and Giggle, specially for the world gig-racing championships. Like other enthusiasts he is constantly adapting and changing the recipes, so by the time you read this, new beers may well have replaced old favourites. They will, however, still be recognizably Ales of Scilly beers.

Real ale is thriving in Cornwall and is becoming easier to find, despite the influence of the big breweries and the so-called pubcos – which bought up many British pubs when the breweries were forced to diversify their holdings following the 1989 Beer Orders Act. Since then, guest beer regulations have been tilted in favour of the big companies, making it difficult for many of the smaller brewers to get their beers into brewery-owned tied houses, or pubco-owned establishments. But more restaurants, bars and pubs that are part of the renaissance of

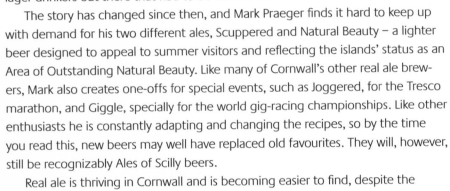

Cornish food and drink are serving real Cornish ales next to lager and the gassy keg imposters. The latter may be successful brands, but their success has little to do with quality, taste and flavour and everything to do with multi-million pound branding and promotional campaigns, funded by the large global conglomerates that own most of the well-known drinks names. The marketing spend, if any, by most of the Cornish breweries is small beer by comparison, making their success even more remarkable.

The growing interest in bottle-conditioned beers is taking Cornish real ale out of a pub-only context into a growing number of off-licences, specialist beer shops, supermarkets, corner shops, farm shops and delicatessens. Skinners, The St Austell Brewery and Sharps all have their own shops, and bottled Spingo can be bought at the Blue Anchor in Helston.

Overall beer sales – by this I mean total beer and lager sales – may be declining, but more than 30 years of successful campaigning by CAMRA, and the commitment and enthusiasm of these Cornish brewers show how they are bucking the trend and this particular niche market is growing.

Real ale is no longer just the preserve of the stereotyped beer enthusiast. Good beer is becoming a fashionable drink in its own right. Brewers are introducing innovative styles and tastes to meet the demand for beers to drink with food – for example, fruit beers, wheat beers, golden ales, stouts and one-off beers for particular events. Like Mark Praeger's summer beer, Natural Beauty, they can reflect the seasons and the circumstances in which they are enjoyed.

This recipe is from Gareth Eddy, a rising star of the Cornish restaurant scene, who cooks in Pescadou in Padstow. Cornish born and bred, he is deeply immersed in the maritime culture around him and is passionate about using the freshest, local ingredients. He uses smoked pollock in this recipe as it is plentiful, a sustainable species, and usually caught as a by-catch. The Clouded Yellow beer is a wheat beer produced by the St Austell Brewery.

## ingredients

### Serves 6

- 600 g risotto rice
- 5 large shallots
- 1 leek (white only)
- 1 chilli (red)
- 1 sprig thyme
- 1 bay leaf
- 1 fennel bulb
- 600 g smoked pollock
- 200 g Cornish butter
- 1 bottle (500 ml) Clouded Yellow beer (or similar wheat beer)

- 3 tbsps olive oil
- 1 litre fish stock
- 1 tsp crushed coriander seeds
- 1 strip diced orange peel
- 1 bunch chives, chopped
- 6 bantam's eggs (or small hen's eggs)
- 1 endive lettuce (for serving)
- sea salt and pepper

**For the dressing:**
- 1 bunch watercress or land cress
- 1 tbsp horseradish (fresh grated, or concentrated creamed)
- 444 ml olive oil

**For the garnish:**
- 12 thin slices panchetta (dried under the grill, bottom shelf until crisp)

# pan-fried smoked cornish pollock risotto cake, with watercress and horseradish dressing, a soft poached bantam's egg and crisp panchetta

*The secret to a good risotto is lots of steam, spankingly good fresh produce, and 18 minutes of hard work.*

This recipe could also be served as a simple risotto, without the trimmings, as soon as it is cooked, but for those who are passionate about risotto this recipe has the benefit that it can be mostly cooked in advance and finished later.

## method

First chop all vegetables and chilli into a fine dice, and warm the saucepan (probably the biggest pan in your kitchen). Bring the fish stock to the boil and poach the pollock for five minutes. Remove and cool slightly before skinning and flaking. Reserve fish stock and keep hot for making the risotto.

*Above:* Gareth Eddy.

Add the olive oil and butter to the hot pan and quickly add the chopped vegetables, orange peel, coriander, thyme and bay leaf, and stir. When the shallots are translucent add the rice and keep stirring.

Add the bottle of Clouded Yellow, stirring constantly until reduced to a syrup.

Then add the hot fish stock, one ladle at a time, stirring constantly, adding the next ladle only when the risotto has absorbed the last ladle. After about 18 minutes the rice should be almost done.

When the rice is just cooked add the flaked smoked pollock and chopped chives,* stir and season and set in a tray lined with clingfilm in a fridge for 3–4 hours. If you are not confident of the ingredients setting in time, put another tray on top and a weight on it. (*At this point the risotto could be served immediately with the watercress sauce.)

Cut the chilled, set risotto cake into desired shapes – squares are effective.

Butter (or brush with olive oil) both sides of the cakes and place them in a hot frying pan, turning them when the edges start to go golden brown.

In a pan half-filled with boiling water, make a whirlpool with a spoon and drop in the eggs one at a time. Poach for three to four minutes depending on how soft you would like the yolk. Place the risotto cake over crisp endive leaves, top with a soft poached egg and garnish with dressing. Top with panchetta crisps.

Take to the table and enjoy with a glass of Clouded Yellow.

*Watercress and horseradish dressing:* Put the watercress, olive oil and horseradish into a blender and blend to a sauce/dressing. Add seasoning and extra horseradish to taste. This should be done as close to serving as possible.

# 15 to your table

If Mrs Beeton started a recipe with 'first catch your cockerel', in Cornwall it could be a case of 'first launch your gig and get out your spade'. This chapter maps out a route around some of the best, and my favourite, specialist retailers, farm shops, farmers' markets and mail order companies, to everything you need to enjoy a superb Cornish taste experience. It proves what Adam Woolfitt and I already knew, when we started this book, that Cornwall produces some fine food that is un-equalled anywhere else in England.

Every week a number of vans can be seen hurtling across the county, from Callington to Bude, Fowey to Helston, or across West Cornwall. They probably be-long to one of the growing number of organic vegetable box schemes, which, for people living in Cornwall, are one of the easiest ways to get some of the county's most interesting and unusual vegetables and other organic foods to their tables.

Box schemes are everywhere, from Rock Organics in Calstock – one of the few growers left in the Tamar Valley – to Nice Organics in West Cornwall and others in between. One of the best known is Cusgarne Organic Vegetable Boxes, run by Greg and Teresa Pascoe just outside Truro, who have been raising organic beef and growing vegetables since 1988. In 1994, fed up with selling to wholesalers and feeling that their vegetables were not always reaching customers in peak condition, the Pascoes started one of Cornwall's first organic vegetable box businesses. 'What I wanted to do was produce an alternative to the supermarkets, and to give people what they want, which is why we offer a complete range,' explained Greg Pascoe.

Customers can choose from more than 80 different vegetables, salads and herbs, from multi-coloured Swiss chard and mizuna to Jerusalem artichokes and celeriac; also listed are organic eggs, and beef from the Pascoes' beef herd; honey

*Right:* Cusgarne Organic Vegetable Boxes – one of the best-known organic vegetable box schemes.

from their own hives; homemade chutneys, and free range chicken from another Cornish organic producer. The vegetables are grown on around 30 acres of the farm, or in polytunnels full of the heavenly scent of late summer tomatoes, peppers, basil, rocket and chilli peppers.

Stepping inside a polytunnel at Cusgarne was an instant reminder of childhood visits to my grandmother, whose vast Edwardian greenhouses overflowed with tomatoes every summer – although who ate them all each year still mystifies me. The heady smell of a freshly picked tomato, the fragrance released as you brush against the plant's leaves, is unique, and a sign that this is real food – carefully grown varieties selected for flavour; a food designed to delight the senses rather than bred to have a tough skin to withstand travelling hundreds of miles, and to have good keeping qualities, enabling it to sit on an artificially lit supermarket shelf for days without losing condition. I include these memories as a reminder of why I am so enthusiastic about some Cornish products – the ones with taste, flavour and quality, that linger in the memory. This is one of the strands of what *Gourmet Cornwall* is about.

So far this book has not distinguished between organic and conventional produce. Most of the businesses I have written about, visited or listed are included because of the quality and distinctiveness of their products. Being organic is often an added bonus. Much of Cornwall's best food and drink would be wonderful whether organic or not. For others, such as wine, organic standards would make it impossible to produce the same end product at an affordable price. While organic producers often like to hold the moral high ground, many other farming and food businesses are just as sustainable and care equally passionately for the Cornish landscape: Charles Gould's and the Lobb

*Left:* Teresa Pascoe.
*Below:* Greg Pascoe.
*Bottom:* Tomatoes in the polytunnel at Cusgarne.
*Page 208:* Roly's Fish; Swiss Chard, and the Gear Farm Shop.
*Page 209: Top:* Dave Webb of Gear Farm Shop. *Middle and bottom:* Lobbs Farm Shop.

brothers' are not the only conventional Cornish farms teeming with birds and wildlife, and maintaining superb trees, hedges and wildflower meadows, but they show how it can be done.

If you want a wide selection of organic produce, much of it made in Cornwall using specially grown Cornish ingredients, try Carleys in Truro, the county's longest-established organic and wholefood

business. The range includes freshly baked bread, vegetables, herbs and salads, and a variety of processed products such as fresh pestos, onion marmalade and chutneys.

The number of dedicated organic outlets is increasing, and one of the newest is Cornish Organics, a farm shop just outside Four Lanes, near Redruth. Started because its owners, Kim and Richard Thomas, realized their business would do better if they sold their organic beef and pork direct to their customers, it has rapidly become a Mecca for local organic produce, including Helsett Farm's yoghurt and ice cream, Barwick Farm dairy produce, organic fruit and vegetables, eggs from Kim Thomas' own flock of Black Rock hens, bread and ready meals made on the farm, and poultry from South Torfrey Farm near Fowey.

Fresh fish takes on a whole new meaning in Cornwall, where much of what you can buy has been caught and landed within the previous 24 hours. Its sparkling, still-briny freshness bears no comparison with the dull, tired-looking specimens displayed in supermarkets. Wet fish shops abound in Cornwall. Many of them also sell by mail order to discerning customers outside the county, guaranteeing a choice of the freshest Cornish fish delivered within 48 hours or less. Try Matthew Stevens' Cornish Collection, Cornish Fish Direct (run by Nick Howell at the Pilchard Works), Fowey Fish, Martin's Seafresh or Quayside Fish in Porthleven. For smoked fish or shellfish Cornish Cuisine, Tregida Smokehouse, Falmouth Bay Oysters and Mark Pender's Isles of Scilly Shellfish Company are among those offering mail-order or online shopping.

High summer is the perfect time to visit one of the growing number of farm shops in Cornwall, which have changed beyond recognition since the mid-1990s. A random, spontaneous visit one June afternoon to Humfrey's Farm Shop, just outside Tregony, offered the following temptations: home-grown globe artichokes; bunches of herbs straight from the garden; Cornish asparagus and strawberries; runner beans, beetroot, broad beans and Cornish new potatoes all freshly dug or picked that morning; local bread, cheese, milk, cream, clotted cream, apple juice and smoked fish. None of that produce would have travelled more than 30 miles to the shop.

One of my personal favourites is the Gear Farm shop, on the Lizard, which opened in 1999 to

sell the farm's organic fruit and vegetables, and meat, apple juice, fish and some other products from local businesses. The co-operative has expanded, changed and moved on since then, and Gear Farm is thriving. More than 90 per cent of the organic vegetables grown on 20 acres of Dave Webb's in-laws' farm goes straight into the shop. When asked for a list of what he grows, he laughed and said 'pretty well everything in the seed catalogue'. During summer and early autumn the shop is a positive cornucopia of fresh salad leaves, tomatoes, herbs, courgettes, beans, peas and so on. It also has a small café, a burgeoning bakery making bread and handmade Cornish pasties each day, and sells local apple juice, ice cream and other dairy products, most of which are organic. It is also an outlet for Roly's Fish – a fish-to-order business delivering fresh fish and shellfish supplied by George and Roly Kirby's boats, *Heart of Oak* and *Marney Lunn*, moored on the nearby Helford River.

One of the few non-organic products stocked at Gear Farm is Davas Farm ewes' milk yoghurt, an example of Dave Webb's passion for good local produce. 'We try not to have lines that are not organic, but when something as good as this comes along, and is obviously produced in a non-intensive way, we would take it.'

The quality of produce and the importance of supporting local producers is a philosophy shared by the Lobb brothers at their farm shop next to the Lost Gardens of Heligan, near Mevagissey. Shopping at Lobbs Farm Shop – which has its own interpretation centre next to the shop, telling the story of the farm through the seasons and the three brothers' philosophy on animal welfare, wildlife and maintaining the countryside – helps to promote an understanding of how good food can be sustainably reared and grown, with provenance, quality and taste, and remaking the connections between the landscape and food production.

An extensive range of the best Cornish produce, including wine and beer, is available here, along with the Lobbs' own-grown meat and vegetables, and other baked goods. This is probably the farm shop with the best range of Cornish, and then Westcountry, produce in the county. Not to be missed if you are in the area.

A word too about other contemporary Cornish foods. Much of this book has concentrated on products that have evolved from centuries of Cornish fishing and agriculture that reflect the landscape and

the climate, and are essentially Cornish because they could only be produced here. But a new generation of food producers emerging in Cornwall illustrates the way in which the Cornish food scene has raised the ante in the last few years, with award-winning, Michelin-starred chefs, gastro pubs and relaxed seaside eating venues that can hold their own against any in the UK. So in addition to cheesemakers and fish smokers, there are new businesses such as the Cornish Chilli Company, Chocolicious and Figgy Dowdy Foods, making their own range of fabulous products that are the perfect addition to any larder or table, from green jalapeno jelly to hand-made chocolates, cakes and preserves with an emphasis on flavour, high volumes of fruit and tastes that capture the freshness of the day the fruit was picked.

All these, plus what we have come to regard as quintessential ingredients, from aged balsamic vinegar to lemon grass and the latest must-have foodie staples, are available. The county is no longer a culinary backwater where essential, but definitely non-Cornish ingredients were once hard to find.

## farmers' markets and country markets

Country Markets have been held across England, Wales and the Channel Islands for almost a century. Originally known as WI Markets, they were set up after the First World War as an outlet for Women's Institute members, and rehabilitated ex-servicemen who had been given allotments on their return from the battlefields, to sell their produce. They have recently been rebranded and updated as Country Markets, and are run independently of the WI. There are 11 in Cornwall, held each week from Callington and Torpoint, to Veryan, Illogan and Penzance, offering a range of the freshest produce – usually bread, cakes, savouries, preserves, eggs, honey, fruit and vegetables according to season. This is the place to find genuinely home-produced Cornish foods such as hevva cake and yeast buns, properly made to family recipes, with no sign of any industrial short cuts, additives or unnecessary preservatives. One of Cornwall's best-kept secrets, each market is different, reflecting local traditions and produce.

Farmers' Markets are a relatively recent phenomenon, but recreate the original markets where farmers sold their produce before our high streets were transformed by the supermarket revolution. Truro, Falmouth, Launceston, Helston and Penzance have thriving weekly Farmers' Markets; others are held fortnightly or once a month. There are at least 15 different venues in Cornwall, although these vary according to the time of year: some are held in market squares, others inside Scout huts and village halls. Don't be put off by the locations: they may not all be brightly lit temples to consumerism, but the food and drink on sale will be far better than the mass-produced, tasteless, woolly textured things that are passed off as food in the giant retail outlets.

For consumers, these markets are a wonderful chance to meet the producers and try the products which the strict guidelines ensure are 'grown, reared, caught, brewed, pickled, baked, smoked or processed by the stallholder', usually within 30 miles of the market. They offer a tempting range of everything from bread to apple juice, cider, cheeses, milk, smoked fish, fruit and vegetables. For embryonic food businesses they are a chance to test the market and get customer feedback on their produce.

Much more high-profile than Country Markets, Farmers' Markets have developed in response to consumers' growing interest in, and passion for, food produced in a way that reflects good animal husbandry, sustainable farming systems and the locality. Their popularity is a reaction to a succession of health-related food scares, such as BSE, and a growing recognition that too much of our food is produced by industrial processes that no longer reflect the seasons and are completely disconnected from our landscape.

One very correct example of how specialist food shops combine the demand for global foods with the new obsession with local produce is the Quay Deli in Falmouth, next to the National Maritime Museum. Not only does this have an excellent selection of salamis, pasta, Thai spices, olive oils and so on, but in addition Emma Mantle stocks a Cornish range covering beer, chilli sauces, cheeses, cider, bottled water and butter.

The shop with the oldest and longest Cornish food provenance is Oughs in Liskeard. Owned by Michael and Margaret Horrell, makers of Cornish Yarg, and tucked away at the bottom of the town, it has been waving a flag for Cornish food

*Left:* The Farmers' Market, Helston.

*Top:* A roadside farm shop near Helston.
*Above:* Spring onions and carrots.
*Right:* Roskilly's fudge, WI marmalade and Cornish honey.

and drink since 1847. In addition to a range of some of the best local products, you can drop in for coffee, a snack or a light lunch.

Food For Thought in Helston is another hidden treasure that is worth the effort to find, and again proudly shows off a selection of Cornish foods. Here jars of Cornish feta are lined up alongside chorizo, Elvas plums and the finest Spanish saffron. This is also the retail home of Cornish Meadow Preserves, otherwise found at Cornwall's farmers' markets, where Tony Marsland makes some of the best jams and preserves in the county – handmade, in small batches, according to products available in season, using no artificial additives, flavourings or preservatives.

There are few parts of the county without either a farm shop or a specialist delicatessen with a good range of Cornish produce, from Kings and the VG Deli in Launceston, Jolly Jack's in Fowey and Latham's Pantry in Wadebridge, to the legendary Di's Dairy and Pantry in Rock. Rick Stein's emporium in Padstow includes a patisserie, wet fish shop and delicatessen, while on Tresco in the Isles of Scilly, the recently rebuilt Tresco Stores has already earned itself the nickname 'Tresco's Harrods'. It is easy to see why. The store has a wide selection of anything and everything that the visitor or resident might need. At the height of the summer season the delicatessen's stocks of about 20 Cornish cheeses are replenished three or four times a week. You can also find Carleys' organic pestos, preserves and sauces, Cornish apple juice, fish, bacon, fairings, bottled water and Tresco beef.

Although many shops now stock a range of Cornish cheeses, make a point of visiting The Cheese Shop in Truro, where Stephen Gunn, Cornwall's only cheese *affineur*, also stocks local bread, apple juices, preserves, eggs, butter, ice cream, locally made preserves and chutneys, and occasionally local ham and sausages.

For those out of the county, there are alternative ways of enjoying this Cornish cornucopia. Retailers such as Oughs, Kings and Jolly Jacks offer online shopping and a range of hampers, both traditional and reflecting contemporary Cornish food, usually with mostly ambient goods that can survive travelling with the rigours of the national carrier system. Try specialist hamper companies such as Food From Cornwall, in West Cornwall, or Seriously Good Gourmet Food, based in North Cornwall and one of the newest arrivals on the scene. Angela Dodds offers a wide cross-section of mostly Cornish produce in what seems like an infinite variety of box schemes, seasonal ideas or selections from organic, fish, dairy and so on. For holidaymakers, what better than to arrive at your Cornish holiday cottage to find a box of freshly gathered local Cornish goodies?

And finally to chocolate. How could anyone finish a feast of the finest food without a brief mention of chocolate and fudge? For Roskillys, on the Lizard, fudge is almost as important as ice cream, made on the farm using their own milk and cream, and there are other exceptional Cornish fudge businesses too. Although cocoa is not grown in Cornwall (yet – except at The Eden Project), like many other parts of Britain the county has its share of aspiring chocolatiers making an impressive range of high-class, exquisite chocolate temptations, from Trenance Chocolates on the Lizard to Chocolicious in Truro, whose rich handmade chocolates are available by mail order.

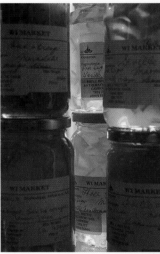

The final word goes to our chocolate chef, Nigel Tabb, who as a bit of a chocoholic himself creates the most astounding handmade chocolates. His recipe, on pages 214–15, gives an idea of the man's talents. Enjoy!

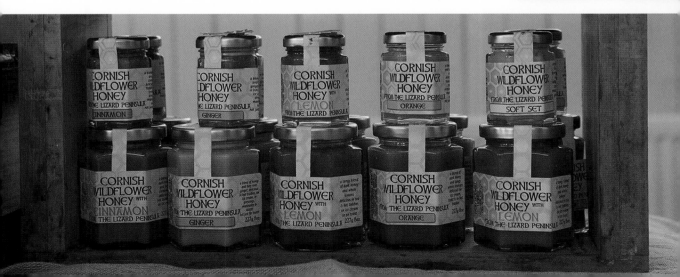

# baked chocolate pudding

This recipe comes from Nigel Tabb at Tabb's Restaurant in Portreath. Nigel is a man who knows his chocolate: he prepares exquisite handmade chocolates for his customers, and puddings such as this.

## ingredients

The success of this pudding depends on using the best quality chocolate – preferably with 70 per cent cocoa content.

*Serves 6*

- 200 g best quality bitter chocolate
- 200 g unsalted butter
- 3 eggs
- 3 egg yolks
- 125 g caster sugar
- 10 g plain flour

## method

Heat the oven to 220°C (gas 7).

Gently melt the chocolate in a microwave, using lots of short bursts rather than one long one as it burns very easily. Alternatively, melt in a bowl over a pan of simmering water.

Melt the butter separately, and mix with the chocolate. Set aside, but keep warm.

In a mixer, beat together the eggs, egg yolks and sugar to form a sabayon. (The mixture will turn nearly white and look like raw meringue).

Using a hand whisk, fold the chocolate mixture into the sabayon, using a gentle twisting motion. Sieve the flour over the top, and fold in very gently with a wooden spoon.

Carefully butter and flour six 10 cm diameter ramekins, or similar baking dishes, and spoon in the mixture so it fills about three-quarters of each dish.

Bake in preheated oven (220°C or gas 7) for 11 minutes. When cooked, carefully release the pudding from the edge of the mould and turn out on to a warm plate. The pudding should be hot but runny in the middle.

Serve with cream or ice cream.

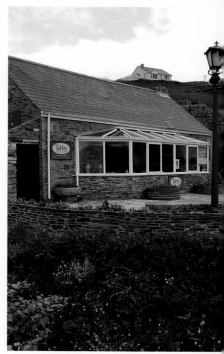

*Top:* Nigel Tabb.
*Above:* Tabb's Restaurant.

*Note:* The success of this recipe depends on having the right sized baking dishes, the oven at the right temperature and timings being precise. If it doesn't work for your oven, adjust the timing by 30 seconds and try again.

# bibliography

Barton, R.M. (ed.) (1972), *Life in Cornwall in the Late Nineteenth Century*. Truro: D. Bradford Barton.

Barty-King, H. (1977), *A Tradition of English Wine: The Story of Two Thousand Years of English Wine Made from English Grapes*. Oxford: Oxford Illustrated Press.

Beamon, S.P. & Roaf, S. (1990), *The Ice-Houses of Britain*. London: Routledge.

Bowley, R.L. (1957), *The Fortunate Islands: The Story of the Isles of Scilly*. Reading: Bowley Publications. Paperback 2004.

Boyd, L. (ed.) (1976), *British Cookery: A Complete Guide to Culinary Practice in the British Isles*. London: Croom Helm.

Butcher, A.L. & Annand, K. F. (eds) (1994), *Recipes and Ramblings: A Taste of Cornwall*. Redruth: Tredinnick Press.

Carew, R. (1953), *The Survey of Cornwall*. Ed. F.E. Halliday. London: Andrew Melrose. *The Survey of Cornwall, 1602*. Exeter: Devon & Cornwall Record Society, 2004.

David, E. (1977), *English Bread and Yeast Cookery*. London: Alan Lane. Penguin Books, 1979.

— (1994), *Harvest of the Cold Months: The Social History of Ice and Ices*. London: Michael Joseph, 1994. Penguin Books, 1996.

Davidson, A. (1979), *North Atlantic Seafood*. London: Macmillan. Totnes: Prospect Books, 2002.

— (2002), *The Penguin Companion to Food*. London: Penguin Books.

Goodchild, D.J. (n.d.), *The Industries of the Tamar Valley*. 1950s paper given to the Horticultural Education Association.

Gray, T. (2000), *The Travellers' Tales: Cornwall*. Exeter: Todd, The Mint Press.

Hall, S. (2001), *The Cornish Pasty*. Bridport: Agre Books.

Hamilton Jenkin, A.K. (1932), *Cornish Seafarers*. London: J.M. Dent & Sons.

— (1933), *Cornwall and the Cornish*. London: J.M. Dent & Sons. Westcountry Books, 2004.

— (1945), *Cornwall and its People*. London: J.M. Dent & Sons. Westcountry Books, 2004.

Hartley, D. (1954), *Food in England*. London: Macdonald. London: Little Brown, 1996.

Hawk, W. (1929), *Agricultural Experiments in Cornwall*. Truro: Netherton & Worth.

Heard, V. (1984), *Cornish Cookery: Recipes of Today and Yesteryear*. Trewirgie: Dyllansow Truran.

Humphries, J. (1996), *The Essential Saffron Companion*. London: Grub Street.

Lewis, J. (2004), *Sovereigns, Madams and Double Whites: Fruit and Flower Pioneers of the Tamar Valley*. Tamar Valley AONB Service.

Liddell, C. & Weir, R. (1995), *Ices: The Definitive Guide*. London: Grub Street.

Martin, C. (1998), *Smuggling Recipes*. St Teath: Bossiney Books.

Martin, E. (1937), *Cornish Recipes Ancient and Modern*. Cornish Federation of Women's Institutes. Truro: Jordan. Truro, 1962, 21st edn.

Mason, L. & Brown, C. (1999), *Traditional Foods of Britain: An Inventory*. Totnes: Prospect Books.

Merrick, Hettie (2005), *Pasties and Cream: Memories and Recipes from a Cornish Childhood*. Redruth: Truran.

Milden, K. (2001), 'Culture of Conversion: Religion and Politics in the Cornish Mining Communities', in *Cornish History*. Published online by the College of St Mark & St John.

Noall, C. (1971), *Smuggling in Cornwall*. Truro: D. Bradford Barton.

— (1972), *Cornish Seines and Seiners: History of the Pilchard Fishing Industry*. Truro: D. Bradford Barton.

Paston-Williams, S. (1993), *The Art of Dining: A History of Cooking and Eating*. London: National Trust Enterprises.

Payton, P. (ed.) (1993), *Cornwall Since the War: The Contemporary History of a European Region*. Redruth: Institute of Cornish Studies & Dyllansow Truran.

Perry, R. (2001), 'Cornwall's Mining Collapse Revisited: An Empirical Survey of Economic Re-adjustment in Late Victorian and Edwardian Cornwall', in *Cornish History*. Published online by the College of St Mark & St John.

Pett, D.E. (2003), *The Cornwall Gardens Guide*. Penzance: Alison Hodge.

Rance, P. (1982), *The Great British Cheese Book*. London: Macmillan. Papermac, 1990.

Rawe, D.R. (1971), *Padstow's Hobby Oss and May Day Festivities*. Padstow: Lodenek Press.

Sears, T. (2002), *The Blue Anchor, Helston, The First 600 Years*. Tim Sears.

Smart, D. (1992), *The Cornish Fishing Industry: A Brief History*. Redruth: Tor Mark Press.

Smylie, M. (2004), *Herring: A History of the Silver Darlings*. London: Tempus, 2004.

Spencer, C. (2002), *British Food: An Extraordinary Thousand Years of History*. London: Grub Street.

Spiers, V. (1996), *Burcombes, Queenies and Colloggetts*. St Dominic, Cornwall: West Brendon Press.

Stein, R. (2004), *Rick Stein's Food Heroes: Another Helping*. London: BBC Books.

Tierney-Jones, A. (2002), *Westcountry Ales*. Tiverton: Halsgrove.

University of Exeter's Centre for Rural Research (2003), *A Study of Food Production, Distribution and Processing in Cornwall and the Isles of Scilly*. Liskeard: Cornwall Taste of the West.

Wilson, C.A. (1973), *Food and Drink in Britain*. London: Constable. Penguin Books, 1984.

Worgan, G.B. (1811), *A General View of the Agriculture of the County of Cornwall*.

Wright, M. (1986), *Cornish Treats*. Penzance: Alison Hodge.

# suppliers and outlets

This is a list of some of the producers and processors featured in *Gourmet Cornwall*, and others that there was no room to include. Most are either retailers or, in the case of farm businesses, welcome visitors. However, it is best to call farm-based producers first if you wish to visit. Food and drink businesses offering a mail order service or online shopping are also shown. Some of the featured businesses do not sell direct to consumers, so are not listed here.

## fish

The fishmonger may be a disappearing species on most high streets, but not in Cornwall. Here is a selection of those selling the best, freshest Cornish fish, shellfish or smoked fish either direct, online or by mail order.

**Atlantis Smoked Fish**, Fore Street, Grampound, T: 01726 883201

**Bude Shellfish**, Lansdown Road, Bude, T: 01288 354727

**The Cornish Collection** (mail order only), M. Stevens & Son, St Ives, T: 01736 799392, W: www.mstevensandson.co.uk

**Cornish Cuisine** (smoked fish, retail and mail order), Islington Wharf, Penryn, Falmouth, T: 01326 376244, W: www.smokedsalmon-ltd.com

**Cornish Fish Direct** (mail order only), The Pilchard Works, Newlyn, T: 01736 332112, W: www.cornishfish.co.uk

**Falmouth Bay Oysters** (mail order only), The Docks, Falmouth, T: 01326 316600, W: www.falmouthoysters.co.uk

**Fowey Fish** (and mail order), 37 Fore Street, Fowey, T: 01726 832422, W: www.foweyfish.com

**Isles of Scilly Shellfish** (mail order only; closed Jan–March), T: 01720 423898, W: www.scillyshellfish.co.uk

**Dennis Knight**, 1 Fore Street, Port Isaac, and 1 Azime Court, Rock, T: 01208 880498/ 862422

**Martins Seafresh** (mail order only), T: 0800 0272066, W: www.martins-seafresh.co.uk

**Pengellys** (and mail order), The Quay, East Looe, T: 01503 262246, and 2 The Arcade, Fore Street, Liskeard, T: 01579 340777

**The Pilchard Works**, Newlyn, T: 01736 332112, W: www.pilchardworks.co.uk

**Quayside Fish Centre** (and mail order),

Porthleven, T: 01326 562008,
W: www.quaysidefish.co.uk

**M. Stevens & Sons**, Back Street East,
St Ives, T: 01736 799392,
W: www.mstevensandson.co.uk

**W. Stevenson & Sons**, Harbour Road,
Newlyn, T: 01736 362982, Market
Place, St Ives, T: 01736 794979,
Wharfside, Wharf Road, Penzance,
T: 01736 331459,
W: www.wstevensonandsons.co.uk

**Tregida Smokehouse** (and mail order),
Trelash, Warbstow, Launceston,
T: 01840 261785,
W: www.tregidasmokehouse.co.uk

**Trelawney Fish** (and mail order), 78 The
Strand, Newlyn, T: 01736 361793, or
0800 5877894 for mail order

## butchers

This is a small selection of the many
Cornish butchers who specialize in
high-quality, local and traditionally
reared meat, with apologies to those not
included due to lack of space:

**Fine Fettle Foods**, Lemon Street Market,
Truro, or Larkhill Farm, St Austell,
T: 01726 72520,
W: www.larkhillfarm.net

**Higher Calenick Farm Butchery**,
Porthkea, nr Truro, T: 01872 271066

**Lenterns Family Butchers**, 1 Chapel
Street, Penzance, T: 01736 363061

**Mr Kittow's Famous Sausage Co.**
(Kilhallon Quality Meats), 1–3 South
Street, Fowey, T: 01726 814926,
W: www.kittowsbutchers.co.uk

**Vivian Olds**, St Just, Penzance, T: 01736
788520, www.vivianolds.co.uk

**Tywardreath Butchers**, 41 Church
Street, Tywardreath, Par,
T: 01726 812051,
W: www.thelocalbutcher.co.uk

**Philip Warren & Son**, Launceston,
T: 01566 772098,
W: www.philipwarrenbutchers.co.uk

Cornish meat producers who sell direct,
either from the farm or at farmers'
markets include:

**Bodinnick Organic**, St Stephen,
St Austell, T: 01726 882421

**Churchtown Farm**, Lanteglos by Fowey,
T: 01726 870375

**Cornish Country Meats**, St Neot,
nr Liskeard, T: 01579 320303

**Primrose Herd**, Busveal, Redruth,
T: 01209 821408

**Rosevinnick Organic Farm**, Lostwithiel,
T: 01726 70588

**Rosuick Organic Farm**, St Martin,
Helston, T: 01326 231302

**Vicarage Farm**, Wendron, Helston,
T: 01326 340484

## dairy products

**Barwick Farm**, Tregony, nr Truro,
T: 01872 530208

**Bradley's Dairy**, Shelton Farm, Delabole,
T: 01840 212578

**The Cheese Shop**, Ferris Town, Truro,
T: 01872 270742

**The Cornish Cheese Co.**, Knowle Cross
Farm, nr Liskeard, T: 01579 363660,
W: www.cornishcheese.co.uk

**Cornish Farmhouse Cheeses**,
Menallack Farm, Treverva, nr Penryn,
T: 01326 340333

**Davas Farm**, Bone Farm, Heamoor,
Penzance, T: 01736 368708

**Gwavas Jersey Farm**, Ruan Minor,
Helston, T: 01326 290232

**Lynher Dairies Cheese Company**,
Lynher Farm, Upton Cross, nr Liskeard,
T: 01579 362244,
W: www.cornishyarg.co.uk

**Pengoon Farm**, Nancegollan, nr Helston, T: 01326 561291, www.pengoon.co.uk

**Priors Green**, Coads Green, nr Liskeard, T: 01579 782547, W: www.lynhervalley.co.uk/priors.htm

**Trewithen Cornish Farm Dairy**, Greymare Farm, Lostwithiel, T: 01208 872214, W: www.cornishfarmdairy.co.uk

**Troytown Farm**, Troytown, St Agnes, T: 01720 422360, W: www.scillylocalfood.org.uk

**Whalesborough Farm Foods Ltd.**, Whalesborough Farm, Marhamchurch, Bude, T: 01288 361317

## ice cream

These ice cream producers sell direct to the public. Their products, and those of other ice cream companies mentioned, are sold through specialist retail outlets, fine food shops, farm shops, etc.

**Callestick Farm Ice Cream**, Callestick, nr Truro, T: 01872 573126, W: www.callestickfarm.co.uk

**Jelberts** (open April–end October), 9 New Road, Newlyn

**Roskilly's Ice Cream**, Tregellast Barton, St Keverne, also tea room, fudge, preserves and other products, T: 01326 280479, W: www.roskillys.co.uk

## baking

**Blue Mango**, Lemon Street Market, Truro, T: 01872 277116

**Cotehele Mill**'s flour is available from the mill, or at the National Trust shop at Cotehele, St Dominick, nr Saltash, T: 01579 352739 (house), 01579 350606 (mill), W: www.nationaltrust.org.uk

**Jolly Jack's**, 24 Fore Street, Fowey, T: 01726 832322, W: www.jollyjacks.co.uk

**The Lizard Pasty Shop** (mail order November–May), Beacon Terrace, The Lizard, T: 01326 290889, W: www.connexions.co.uk/lizardpasty/index.htm

**Lostwithiel Bakery**, 2 Quay Street, Lostwithiel, T: 01208 873233

**Lydia's Cottage Industry**, Carnkie, Redruth, T: 01209 217352

**H.M. Pearce**, Station Road, Kelly Bray, T: 01579 383362

**Promises and Piecrusts**, Truthwell, nr Penzance, T: 01736 711764

**St Martin's Bakery**, Moo Green, St Martin's, Isles of Scilly, T: 01720 423444, W: www.stmartinsbakery.co.uk

**Trescowthick Craft Bakery**, Newlyn East, Newquay, T: 01637 830598

## apple juice and cider

Cornwall has only a few apple juice and cidermakers, but those listed below are open to the public.

**Cornish Orchards**, Westnorth Manor Farm, Duloe, T: 01503 263373, W: www.cornishorchards.co.uk

**The Cornish Cyder Farm**, Penhallow, T: 01872 573356, W: www.thecornishcyderfarm.co.uk

**Haye Farm Cider**, St Veep, Lerryn, Lostwithiel, T: 01208 872250

**Helford Creek**, Mudgeon Vean, St Martin, nr Helston, T: 01326 231341, W: www.helfordcreek.co.uk

## vineyards

The following Cornish vineyards are open to the public; other private or semi-commercial vineyards are not open to visitors. Most sell wine direct to customers, but it is advisable to contact growers before visiting. Cornish wines are also available in many off-licences and specialist shops.

**Camel Valley Vineyard**, Nanstallon, nr Wadebridge, T: 01208 77959, W: www.camelvalley.com

**Lambourne Vineyard**, Ruan High Lanes, nr Truro, T: 01872 501212, W: www.lambournevineyard.co.uk

**Oak Valley Wines**, Bosue, nr Mevagissey, T: 01726 843159, W: www.cornwallwines.co.uk

**Pemboa Vineyard**, Pemboa, Helston, T: 01326 563116

**Polmassick Vineyard**, St Ewe, nr Mevagissey, T: 01726 842239

**St Martin's Vineyard**, St Martin's, Isles of Scilly, T: 01720 422863, W: www.stmartinsvineyard.co.uk

## beer

Cornish real ales are available in a growing number of Cornish pubs, and also further away. The easiest way to buy these is as bottled, conditioned beer in off-licences, some supermarkets and specialist retailers such as farm shops and delicatessens. More information about Cornish micro-breweries is available on the Cornwall CAMRA website, www.carnmenellis.demon.co.uk.

**The Blue Anchor** (sells bottled Spingo) 50 Coinagehall Street, Helston, T: 01326 562821, W: www.duchy.net/index.htm

**St Austell Brewery** (retail shop and visitor centre), Trevarthian Road, St Austell, T: 01726 66022, W: www.staustellbrewery.co.uk

**Sharps Brewery** (retail shop), Rock, nr Wadebridge, T: 01208 862121, W: www.sharpsbrewery.co.uk

**Skinners** (retail shop and visitor centre), Riverside View, Newham, Truro, T: 01872 271885, W: www.skinners.brewery.co.uk

## farm shops

For fruit, vegetables, meat and other Cornish products. Please note some farm shops are not open all year round.

**Bill and Flo's Farm Shop**, Lelant, St Ives, T: 01736 798885

**Boddingtons PYO**, Avalon Gardens, Mevagissey, T: 01726 842346, W: www.boddingtonsberries.co.uk

**Chyreen Fruit Farm and PYO**, Carnon Downs, Truro, T: 01872 862317, W: http://www.chyreen.ukf.net/

**Cornish Organics**, Four Lanes, nr Redruth, T: 01209 215789

**Gear Farm Shop**, St Martin, Helston, T: 01326 221150

**Humfreys Farm Shop**, Tregony, nr Truro, T: 01872 530417

**Lobbs Farm Shop** (next to the Lost Gardens of Heligan), St Ewe, nr St Austell, T: 01726 844411

**Mitchell Fruit Garden**, Mitchell, nr Newquay, T: 01872 510774

**Porteath Bee Centre**, St Minver, nr Port Isaac, T: 01208 863718, W: www.porteath-beecentre.co.uk

**Richards of Cornwall Farm Shop**, Carwin Farm, Loggans, Hayle, T: 01736 757888

**Trevaskis Farm Shop**, Gwinnear Road, Connor Downs, nr Hayle, T: 01209 713931

**Trevelyan Farm Shop**, Perranuthnoe, Marazion, T: 01736 710410

**Trevilley Farm Shop**, Lane, Newquay, T: 01637 872310

## vegetable boxes

**Cusgarne Organic Vegetables**,
Cusgarne Wollas, Cusgarne, nr Truro,
T: 01872 865922

**Nice Organics**, The Old Dairy, Sancreed,
nr Penzance, T: 01736 810033,
W: www.niceorganics.co.uk

**Rock Organics**, Calstock, Church Lane,
Calstock, T: 01822 832178

## specialist food shops and delicatessens

**Carleys**, 34–6 St Austell Street, Truro,
T: 01872 277686, www.carleys.co.uk

**Di's Dairy and Pantry**, Rock Road, Rock,
T: 01208 863531, W: www.rockinfo.
co.uk/rock/disdairy.html

**Food For Thought**, 3a Church Street,
Helston, T: 01326 563785, W: www.
cornishmeadow.com/page4.html

**Jolly Jack's** (also hampers), 24 Fore
Street, Fowey, T: 01726 832322,
W: www.jollyjacks.co.uk

**Kings** (also hampers), 9 White Hart
Arcade, Launceston, T: 01566 774743,
W: www.kingsdeli.co.uk

**Oughs** (also hampers), 9 Market Street,
Liskeard, T: 01579 343253,
W: www.oughs.co.uk

**Quay Deli**, Discovery Quay, Falmouth,
T: 01326 210808

**D.L. Tregenza**, 6 Greenmarket,
Penzance, T: 01736 362804

**The Tresco Stores**, Tresco, Isles of Scilly,
T: 01720 422806

**VG Deli**, 6–8 Church Street, Launceston,
T: 01566 779494

## hampers

(See also specialist food shops and delicatessens)

**Food From Cornwall**, Hilary Wood,
T: 01209 860496,
W: www.foodfromcornwall.co.uk

**Harmony Hampers**, 7 Lansdowne Road,
Callington, T: 0870 243 0547,
W: www.harmony-hampers.co.uk

**Seriously Good Gourmet Food**,
21 Glynn Road, Padstow, T: 0870 241
7027, www.seriously-good.co.uk

## farmers' markets and country markets

At the time of going to press, markets
were held in the following locations, but
these change frequently. It is best to ask
for local information.

### country markets

**Callington**, Scout Headquarters, every
Wednesday

**Helston**, The Guildhall, every Friday

**Illogan**, Chapel Hall, every Tuesday

**Launceston**, Guild Hall, every Tuesday

**Liskeard**, The Long Room Public Hall,
every Friday

**Penzance**, St John's Hall, every Thursday

**Perranporth**, Memorial Hall, every Friday

**Roseland**, Memorial Hall, Portscatho,
every Friday

**Torpoint**, Silver Band Hut, every Tuesday

**Veryan**, Veryan Parish Hall, every Friday

**Wadebridge**, Town Hall, every Thursday

### farmers' markets

**Bodmin**, Public Rooms, 4th Saturday
of the month

**Callington**, Town Hall, 2nd and 4th
Friday of the month

**Carnon Downs**, Village Hall, last
Saturday of the month

**Falmouth**, The Moor, every Tuesday

**Helston**, The Guildhall, every Monday

**Launceston**, Town Hall, every Tuesday

**Liskeard**, Keep Fit Hall, Market Road,